Women
War
Heroines

Women
War
Heroines

GEORGE AND ANNE FORTY

ARMS AND
ARMOUR

Arms and Armour Press
An Imprint of the Cassell Group
Wellington House, 125 Strand, London WC2R 0BB

Distributed in the USA by Sterling Publishing Co. Inc.,
387 Park Avenue South, New York, NY 10016-8810.

British Library Cataloguing-in-Publication Data:
a catalogue record for this book is available from the British Library

ISBN 1-85409-397-5

Designed and edited by DAG Publications Ltd. Designed by David
Gibbons; edited by John Gilbert; printed and bound in Great Britain.

Jacket Illustrations

Front: Kenau Hasselaar on the ramparts of Haarlem, a painting by
Johannes Hinderikus Egenberger and Barend Wijnveld, Jr., signed and
dated 1854. (Frans Hals Museum). **Back, top**: 'Heroism of the Maid of
Saragossa', from *Cassell's Illustrated History of England*. **Back,
bottom**: Red Army tank commander Maria Vasilyevna Oktyabrskaya
who was posthumously awarded 'Heroine of the Soviet Union',
bought her own tank to fight against the 'Hitlerists' after they
had killed her husband. (Central Armed Forces Museum)

Contents

Introduction 7

Chapter 1. The Matriarchs 9
Boudicca, the warrior queen.....10
Grace of the cropped hair 16

Chapter 2. Protecting the
  Home..................................19
Lady Mary Bankes 19
Charlotte Stanley, Countess of
  Derby....................................23
Lady Blanche Arundel 25
Kenau Hasselaar, defender of
  Haarlem................................25

Chapter 3. The Visionaries ...28
Joan of Arc 28
Agustina, the Maid of
  Saragossa 32
Louise Michel, the Red Virgin...37

Chapter 4. The Patriots 42
Renée Bordereau, heroine of
  La Vendée..............................42
Heroines of the American
  Civil War 46
Belle Boyd, 'La Belle Rebelle' ...49

Chapter 5. Following the
  Loved One 56
Mother Ross, dragoon and
  sutleress 57
Mary Schellenck.......................61
Loreta Velázquez 63
Susanna Dalbiac and Lady
  Juana Smith, heroines
  undisguised 68
Margaret Corbin, Fanny Doyle
  and Molly Pitcher – women at
  the guns................................74
Anita Garibaldi........................78

Chapter 6. Women at Sea.....85
Mary Anne Talbot....................86
Mary Read 91
Anne Bonny 94
Hannah Snell, the brave
  marine..................................95

Chapter 7. Eternal
  Tomboys 101
Catalina de Erauso, the ensign
  nun....................................101
Sarah Taylor, the Manchester
  heroine 103

CONTENTS

A Prussian heroine, Anne
Sophia Detzliffin..................106

Deborah Sampson Gannett,
revolutionary roldier 108

The Fernig Sisters, a pair of
heroines..............................112

Thérèse Figueur, the carefree
dragoon 115

**Chapter 8. In Father's
Footsteps 117**

Phoebe Hessel, the little
drummer............................118

Alexandrine Barreau, the
Tarn grenadier 120

**Chapter 9. The
Professionals 122**

Flora Sandes: Nashi
Engleskinja, 'Our English-
woman' 122

Yashka, peasant, exile and
soldier...............................128

**Chapter 10. The
Opportunists....................134**

James Barry, an officer and
a gentleman 134

Dorothy Lawrence 139

Chapter 11. Spies...............146

Chevalier d'Eon....................147

Mata Hari.............................151

Edith Louisa Cavell 152

Marie-Madeleine Fourcade......152

Christine Granville, GM, OBE,
Croix de Guerre 153

Yvonne Claire Cerneau –
'Jacqueline' 157

**Chapter 12. To Fight or
not to Fight....................159**

British servicewomen 159

American servicewomen 161

Women soldiers worldwide 163

**Chapter 13. Fact or
Fiction?..........................166**

Jenny Cameron.......................166

Lucy Brewer, leatherneck or
liar?...................................169

Colonel Sir Victor Barker, DSO
173

**Chapter 14. Women Warriors
in Song and Verse............175**

Acknowledgements............186

Index..................................187

Introduction

Throughout the ages, the battlefield, the uniform and the weapons of the soldier have generally been regarded as strictly male preserves; however, we shall endeavour to show that in fact this is very far from the truth. There have always been brave, determined and adventurous women, who have fought in battle just as capably as men, and their stories make fascinating reading. The reasons why they have decided to take part in bloody combat, and if necessary to kill other human beings, are varied and complex. In this book we investigate the lives of a number of these 'women warriors'; and in an attempt to explain the root causes that have made these women so different from the majority of their sex, we have grouped them under various classifications. Apart from a few of the more single-minded individuals among them, there is inevitably a good deal of overlap between these categories.

It would be convenient of course simply to distinguish these fighting women as those who disguised themselves as men and those who fought openly as women. Although the latter group have been courageous and indomitable, one cannot help but be more fascinated by the former, who have, for the record, included a major-general, miscellaneous officers, NCOs and men of all ranks, drummer boys and powder monkeys, sailors and marines, even pirates and highwaymen! In these days of strict and searching medical examinations of recruits, it is difficult to imagine how these adventurous females ever managed to enlist. In previous centuries, however, there were no such examinations and medical aid was extremely rough and ready. Add to this the fact that clothing then was a good deal thicker and looser than worn today and it is easier to understand how a young woman could pass for a slimly built, beardless youth. Nor were people all that fussy about personal hygiene. Few ever bothered to do more than rinse their hands and face; undressing to get washed was unheard of on the battlefield. More difficult to conceal must have been the performance of normal bodily functions and of course menstruation, but the women all managed somehow.

Undoubtedly, it helped enormously to have some kind of 'protector' in the know, as did the limited privacy of officer's quarters when compared to the open public existence of the private soldier. Occasional discovery usually came if the woman was wounded and unable to prevent the all-too-obvious feminine parts of her anatomy from being unveiled. Our accolade for the cleverest disguise goes to Hannah Snell, the woman who served as a marine, living within the confines of the lower deck on a British man-o'- war; that must have taken courage, skill and guile (or just sheer cheek !) of the very highest order!

How different all these feminine warriors were to the modern woman, who today considers it her right to be accepted into any male role – even to the extent of combat duty. In many countries women are actively serving with distinction on land, sea and air.

Although with the passing of time, conventions on quite fundamental issues do change dramatically, the idea of allowing women to fight in battle seems hard for many Western males to contemplate. Future generations may well look back on our prejudices over employing women in combat and wonder what all the fuss was about!

From Boudicca to Flora Sandes, from Joan of Arc to Yashka Botchkareva, from the brave Dame Mary Bankes to the intrepid Lady Smith, women have continually been an inspiration to their menfolk on the battle-field, urging them on to greater feats of bravery and fortitude. Perhaps their example gives lie to the fears of those who feel that men would be too busy looking after the women to fight properly – certainly we have found little to substantiate this opinion.

We have not tried to compile an encyclopaedia of all the women who fought in battle; clearly their numbers are legion and it would take a huge book to do them justice. It has been an interesting topic to research, and we hope it will prove equally interesting to read. Truly, the female of the species can be as deadly as the male!

George and Anne Forty
Bryantspuddle
1997

CHAPTER I

The Matriarchs

O nce upon a time, so the story goes, the women of ancient China, discontented with their unequal share in the running of the country, rose in rebellion. Their revolt so very nearly succeeded that the shaken emperor, and his male advisers, decided to take drastic action to ensure it could never happen again. Consequently he decreed that in future the feet of all female babies would be bound in such a way as to prevent them ever again growing up to fight in armed combat.

The ancients of the Western world, however, held very different views indeed. They even had their own goddesses of War, such as the Egyptian Neith, the Greek Enyo and the Roman Bellona, who used to drive the battle chariot for her husband Mars. Perhaps the most famous of the ancient women warriors were the Amazons who inhabited Cappadocia in Asia Minor. They were forbidden to have any dealings with men, except on certain days of the year when they visited the surrounding tribes in order to become pregnant. No males were permitted to live in their society, so any male babies were strangled at birth. The word 'Amazon' comes from two Greek words meaning 'wanting a breast', because young Amazonian girls had their right breast burnt off so that, when they grew to maturity, they would be better able to draw a bow or hurl a spear. Homer tells of these women who were bred '… not in idleness, nor spinning, but in exercises of war, such as hunting and riding'. He also wrote of them invading Lycia, where they were defeated by Bellerophon; of them being allies of Priam in the Trojan Wars; and even of their invading Attica, where they were finally beaten by Theseus, who then married their queen, Antiope. Mythical characters they may have been, but they had their living origins in the warlike women of Scythia, who fought in battle alongside their menfolk.

The people of northern Europe – the Goths, Vandals and Germans – who overran Europe during the decline of the Roman Empire, recognised their own mythological women warriors in the shape of the fearsome Valkyries, '... those dread maids, whose hideous yell maddens the battle's bloody swell'. These formidable women were believed to play a leading part in every battle. Mounted on powerful horses, with winged helmets and enormous swords, they rode wildly over the field of combat, selecting those heroes destined by Odin for slaughter, and then led them to the paradise of the brave – Valhalla. Most other races have at one time or another held similar beliefs, including the ancient Britons who prayed to Andate, goddess of Victory.

Given that ancient Western goddesses were expected to be warlike, what about mere mortals? Certainly, there is considerable evidence that in earlier times, a woman of the ruling classes was generally allowed to inherit. This meant that the daughter – or widow – of a chieftain could, on the death of her father, or husband, find herself the matriarch and head of her tribe and thus expected to lead them into battle. The same still applied, to a limited degree, in the Middle Ages when, during the Crusades, many wives of knights and barons who had accompanied their lords to the Holy Lands took over command when their husbands were killed. Not until monarchs ceased automatically to lead their armies into battle, did this practice really come to an end. Eventually a woman's role in the family, apart from the odd exception, changed to one of support in the home and subservience, in law, to the males in her life.

Boudicca, the warrior queen

The most famous of all British fighting women, perhaps the greatest of the matriarchs, was Boudicca, the warrior queen of the Iceni. Her name is the feminine of Bodiccus and is derived from the Welsh 'budd', meaning 'victory', the equivalent of the later Victoria.

Boudicca was the daughter of Cadalla, king of the Brigantes, and the wife of Prasutagus, king of the Iceni, a people who lived in the area that is now Norfolk and Suffolk. Prasutagus and Boudicca had two daughters, whose names remain unknown, and a son who died young, and they seem to have led a reasonably contented life together.

The Iceni had made terms with the invading Romans as early as the time of Caesar, but they were still a powerful and warlike race and their queen was a striking example of these handsome and fearless people. Taller than average, she had bright chestnut hair which hung down to her waist, a commanding presence and a vivid personality. Dio describes her as having 'a huge frame, a terrifying aspect and a harsh voice', which is probably exaggerating her physical appearance, but she was clearly a formidable woman. One gets a very vivid impression of her warlike bearing from the statue by Thomas Thornycroft called *Boudicca and her Daughters*, which stands beside the Thames at Westminster. Depicting her in a chariot accompanied by her daughters, addressing her followers just before battle, it was described by *The Times*, when it was unveiled: '... Her face and attitude are instinct with commanding grandeur; she orders the extinction of her foes; she appeals to her people not in frenzy and tears, in tones heart-stirring and eloquent no doubt, but with more pride than rage in them, and her haughty spirit does not dream of defeat.'

In AD 48, the harsh policies of the Romans had caused a revolt which was led by the Iceni; but this insurrection was quickly and ruthlessly dealt with. Prasutagus was allowed to remain king of the Iceni because he became an ally of Rome; consequently he had a reasonably long and prosperous reign. When he died in the year 59 he was very wealthy. He tried to safeguard his family fortune by leaving half of his estate to the Roman emperor; the remainder was divided between his two daughters, his widow inheriting nothing.

However, Catus Decimus, the Roman procurator fiscal of Britain, had other ideas; collecting a force of soldiers, he marched against the Iceni and proclaimed that everything they possessed was to go to the emperor. Applying this ruling to the entire kingdom and not just the late king's estate, he confiscated the lands and property of all the Icenian nobles and carried off many of the people as slaves. His soldiers went even further at the palace where they bound and flogged Boudicca and raped her daughters in her presence.

One can imagine how she felt, her loved ones outraged, her possessions looted and she, the queen, treated as a slave. This was like a red rag to a bull and her tribe rose in open revolt.

Colchester in AD 55 was a newly built Roman town which had grown up around the original military camp. Plans were afoot, and foundations dug, for a vast new temple, causing great resentment among the local community, so that when Boudicca went on the warpath she had no difficulty in finding enthusiastic supporters. Addressing them, spear in hand, she declared: 'Some of you may have been duped by the Romans' tempting promises. Now you have learned the difference between foreign tyranny and the free life of your ancestors. Have we not suffered every shame and humiliation?' It is a measure of her personality that she was unanimously elected as war leader and proved her worth by welding the notoriously individualistic Celts into a strong force.

The Roman governor, Caius Suetonius Paulinus, and the majority of the garrison troops, were busily engaged in the conquest of the island of Mona (Anglesey), and the north-western mainland of Wales when the Iceni revolt began. Anglesey and Wales had long been a stronghold of the Druid religion. Since the Roman conquest these parts had become a refuge for many rebels and the occupation forces were determined to bring this troublesome region under control.

When they reached the Menai Straits, the Romans had to build flat-bottomed boats to carry their infantry across – the cavalry swimming alongside their horses. To their surprise and dismay they were opposed not only by the Druids but also by hordes of fierce men and fanatical women, dressed in black, with dishevelled hair, shrieking curses and brandishing torches. The superstitious soldiers likened them to the Furies and took a lot of urging forward; Suetonius obviously had his hands full trying to subdue this formidable enemy alliance.

Boudicca, taking advantage of this diversion, managed to recruit followers from most of the tribes in south-east England. Dio says that her army numbered 120,000; and considering the fact that Celtic warriors took their entire families and livestock with them when they went to war, the size of the vengeful army must have been enormous. Boudicca waited until Suetonius was fully engaged with the final attack on Mona, and then led her army into the field. Her first objective was Colchester, and although the garrison made a desperate two-day stand in the Temple of Claudius, they were overwhelmed and all were massacred.

The nearest Roman troops were now the XX Legion, stationed at Lincoln about 120 miles away; learning of the revolt they marched with all speed to deal with it. Boudicca detached part of her army to meet this threat and the forces clashed at Godmanchester.

The celebrated Roman historian, Tacitus, was in Britain at the time of the revolt and gives this account of the battle: 'The victorious Britons went out to meet Petilius Cerialis, legate of the legion, who was advancing to the rescue. They routed the legion and slaughtered all his infantry. Cerialis himself escaped with the cavalry, and found shelter behind the defences of his camp.'

What a fillip this victory, over a large and well-disciplined body of Roman soldiers, must have been for Boudicca. Now the only Roman force in Britain which was capable of stopping her was the army of Suetonius, and he was too far away to be an immediate threat. Catus Decimus, whose greed had caused all the trouble, took the opportunity to escape across to Gaul.

Boudicca and her victorious raggle-taggle army pressed on, this time in the direction of London. Suetonius had by now heard of the insurrection, but his army was very tired after its successful Welsh campaign and still, of course, miles away. Nevertheless, he wasted no time and set out with his cavalry for London, ordering his infantry to follow with all speed. It would take the infantry of the XIV and XX Legions, who had been with him in Wales, over two weeks to reach London, so he sent messengers to the II Legion at Gloucester, ordering them to meet him en route. For some unaccountable reason, the officer in charge, Poenius Postumus, the camp prefect (the legate being absent) refused to obey this order and kept his legion in camp. This deliberate refusal to obey orders was virtually unheard of in an army as well disciplined as that of Rome; and since Poenius later killed himself, no explanation of this strange action has ever been discovered. Thus Suetonius reached London with just his cavalry force of about 1500 men. He quickly realised that he could do nothing against the enormous horde of Celts who were even then sacking the doomed town, so he decided to withdraw along the route he had come, to meet up with his infantry. By doing so he would have a balanced force which might then at least have a chance of defeating the rebels.

His action left thousands of London civilians defenceless and they were slaughtered without mercy. Tacitus says that Boudicca's soldiers were not interested in taking prisoners to sell as slaves, 'but only in killing by the sword, the gibbet, by fire and the cross, like men soon about to pay the penalty and meanwhile snatching at instant vengeance'. Then, instead of following Suetonius, the horde turned on St Albans, where they repeated a similar orgy of killing, burning and pillage.

13

Boudicca's triumph, however, was to be short-lived; her army was ill-organised and difficult to keep under control, and she must have realised that by giving Suetonius time to concentrate his forces, she was running a tremendous risk. Not that he would be able to muster anything like equal numbers, but they would be disciplined veteran soldiers well used to battle against the odds and ready to avenge the reputed number of 70,000 Roman citizens slaughtered in London, Colchester and St Albans. And so the two sides approached the final battle.

The actual location of this battle has never been accurately determined; it has been suggested, however, that Veronae (High Cross), where Watling Street crossed the Fosse Way, was the most likely spot. Suetonius was able to select his position, as Tacitus explains: 'He chose a position in a narrow defile, protected from behind by forest. Here he could be sure that there would be no enemy except in front and where an open plain gave no cover for ambushes.'

Before the battle, Boudicca passed up and down in her chariot, exhorting her warriors to remember all the Romans had done to them and in particular to avenge her personal wrongs and those of her daughters. She went from tribe to tribe, endeavouring to stir their blood-lust, countering any argument by stressing that it was customary for Britons to fight under the leadership of a woman. Tacitus quotes her words:

'But now it is not a woman descended from noble ancestry but as one of the people that I am avenging lost freedom, my scourged body, the outraged chastity of my daughters. Roman lust has gone so far that not our very persons, not even age or virginity are left unpolluted. But heaven is on the side of the righteous vengeance; a legion which dared to fight has perished; the rest are hiding themselves in their camp, or thinking anxiously of flight. They will not sustain even the din and the shout of so many thousands, much less our charge and our blows. If you weigh well the strength of the armies and the causes of war, you will see that in this battle you must conquer or die. This is a woman's resolve; as for men, they may live to be slaves.'

Suetonius also spoke to his troops. He told them to ignore the noise and the empty threats of the 'savages', who were untrained for battle and would soon break and run when they found themselves up against the weapons and courage of real soldiers who had beaten them many times before, adding that there were many women in the enemy ranks apart from Boudicca and her daughters. He reminded his men that few of them would win battle honours, but promised glory would be theirs as they were a small band fighting against huge odds – for the honour of the Roman army. He instructed them to keep in close formation, to throw their javelins and then press on, using their shield bosses to batter down the enemy and their swords to kill them. He exhorted them not to think of the booty but to drive on: 'Win the battle and you will win everything.'

As they advanced, the Britons brushed aside the Roman skirmishers who were harassing them, and began their long charge up the incline towards the legionaries who were formed at the top of the slope. Each legionary had a light javelin in addition to his short broadsword and shield; the front rank hurled their javelins when the onrushing Celts were about forty yards away. They then threw a second javelin and side-stepped so that the second rank could fling their two spears. This continued with practised precision until the enemy was within ten yards. The legions then advanced in close ranks, raising their long rectangular shields and drawing their short swords, adopting a wedge-shaped formation to break through the advancing mass of British tribesmen. Shuffling forward, they gradually drove the Celts back down the hill. Boudicca was everywhere, trying to urge on her rebels, but the solid phalanx of Roman soldiers hammered away at the massed Britons who were already reeling from the deadly barrage of spears, and slowly hemmed them in against the press of wagons containing the women, children and supplies that were following close behind. There was no escape and when the cavalry came charging in from the flanks, the rout was complete.

It has been estimated that over 80,000 Britons were killed for the loss of only 400 legionaries. The battle put a complete end to the revolt and finally established Roman supremacy in Britain. 'It was a glorious victory, like those of the old days,' wrote Tacitus.

And what of Boudicca? She and her two daughters disappeared from the battlefield and, according to historians, managed to get back to their own area before taking poison. It was a sad ending. Her grave has never been found, but the memory of her courageous exploits lives on, earning her a permanent place in British history.

Grace of the cropped hair

From very early times the various Irish chieftains, who jealously guarded their separate kingdoms, were a law unto themselves, fighting and murdering one another for the title High King of Ireland. It was not until the twelfth century, however, that England became involved with the disputes.

In 1166, Diarmait Mac Murchada, deposed king of Leinster, escaped to England to seek allies to help him regain his throne. One of his main recruits was Richard FitzGilbert de Clare, nicknamed Strongbow. In return for his support, Strongbow was made heir to the throne of Leinster and was promised Diarmait's daughter Aife in marriage. Diarmait and his allies landed in Ireland in 1169, took Dublin and reconquered Leinster. When Diarmait died a year later, Strongbow inherited as promised. On hearing this, Henry II of England, who had been granted the right to rule Ireland by Pope Adrian IV, decided to invade the country, now threatening to become a rival power, and to subdue the chieftains. At the end of his successful campaign, Henry was accepted by the Irish chieftains as their overlord, and permitted Strongbow to keep Leinster as a fiefdom.

In the sixteenth century rebellion and bloodshed were still a constant feature of Irish life. One of the most famous rebels of the period was Grace O'Malley (Graine Ni Mhaille), nicknamed 'Grace of the cropped hair'. She was the daughter of Dubhdro Ni Mhaille, a chieftain of county Galway, whose castle Carraig an Chabhlaigh stands in Clew Bay. His territory included the wild and rugged coastline with its hundreds of rocky inlets and the western isles. He was basically a privateer, living a very comfortable life on the proceeds of his sorties at sea, and Grace often accompanied him as a child. They attacked any ships which came anywhere near their territory along the western coast, not only English shipping but also those of rival clans.

When her father died, Grace, ignoring any prior claim that her younger brother might have imagined he had, took over as chief of the O'Malleys. This high-spirited and dauntless woman became pirate queen of the west coast, leading daring and dangerous forays on local shipping from her remote castle in its rocky bay. Familiar with every inch of her territory, she would appear – as if out of nowhere – from a concealed inlet, attack the surprised victim and then slip quickly back into yet another hidden cove. She married twice. Her first husband was Domhnall an Chogaidh O'Flaithearta (O'Flaherty) of Connaught and they had two sons.

On the death of her first husband she married an Englishman, Sir Richard Burke. His ancestors, the de Burgos, had gone to Ireland with Strongbow and settled there permanently, taking an Irish name – Mac William Eughter – and learning both the language and the customs. Sir Richard and Grace had a son named Theobald, who inherited his mother's love for the sea and ships and became known as Theobald of the Ships.

In 1568, Sir Henry Sidney, acting as Elizabeth I's Lord Deputy, visited Ireland and appointed Edward Fitton as first President of Connaught. He was to rule from the town of Galway on behalf of the queen. Unfortunately Sidney could not have chosen a more unsuitable man for the job. Sir Edward, cruel, vicious and much detested, was the direct cause of a rebellion led by the Burke family. When Sidney heard of the insurrection he returned to Ireland with a strong force. He found the town of Galway deserted as most of its inhabitants had gone to join the Burkes.

After protracted negotiations, the rebel leaders finally consented to submit to royal authority. Grace, too, reluctantly agreed, for the time being, to stop her attacks on British ships. Sir Henry met Grace in 1576 and wrote afterwards, 'There came to me a most famous feminine sea-captain, called Grany-I-Mallye, and offered her service unto me, wheresoever I would command her, with three galleys and two hundred fighting men, wither in Ireland or Scotland. She brought with her her husband, for she was, as well by sea as by land, more than a master's mate with him.... This was the most notorious woman in all the coasts of Ireland.'

Grace, however, very soon became bored with the inactivity, and again began her harassment of English ships. In 1577 she was captured and brought to Dublin by the Earl of Desmond. Her husband Richard accompanied her and continued to plead for her release, which came the following year. When the sheriff of Galway sent a large naval force to besiege her castle of Rockfleet, Grace and her ships routed the fleet completely. On another occasion, when a man named Theobald Dillon invaded her territory, Grace captured him and was about to have him killed, but Richard persuaded her to let him go. She continued her raids on English shipping and, showing even more daring, was raiding the isle of Arran when she was again captured. Sir Richard Bingham, the new president of Connaught, decided to have her executed, describing her as 'a notable traitoress and nurse of all the rebellions in the province for forty years'. Once more she was released on the intervention of her faithful husband.

In 1588, Grace attacked some of the routed ships of the Spanish Armada. Queen Elizabeth, delighted with the news of the action, invited her to visit the court in London, where her son Theobald was created 1st Viscount Mayo.

After the death of her husband Grace retired to her castle with her followers and a gift from the queen of a thousand cows and horses. Even now she was unable to resist the lure of the sea, and continued to make the occasional sally, remaining a thorn in England's flesh. In 1595 she wrote to Lord Burghley, Lord High Treasurer of England, asking for the restitution of her late husband's confiscated estates, but this was never granted. She died a few years later, in poverty, and was buried on Clare Island, the headquarters of her naval activities.

CHAPTER 2

Protecting the Home

In nature a wild animal, be it male or female, will usually defend its lair against all comers. This is especially true of a mother defending her young. No matter how weak she may appear, she will invariably protect her offspring with claws, teeth, horns or tusks. The same is applicable to humans. It was Sir Edward Coke, in the sixteenth century, who first coined the much misquoted phrase that 'a man's house is his castle'. Similarly, most people will defend their homes against enemies, be they soldiers of an invading army, robbers, burglars or even bailiffs intent upon evicting them. Here, too, women are just as pugnacious as men in defending their homes and families.

Most of our examples in this category are from the ugly Civil War period, fought in England from 1642 to 1649, when Oliver Cromwell and his Roundheads laid siege to castles and country houses belonging to the supporters of the king, and laid many of them waste. We tell the stories of three courageous women who, in the absence of their husbands, defended their family homes.

Some women even went a step further than this and defended not just their private homes but also, through their inspiration and example, those of their neighbours as well.

Lady Mary Bankes

Lady Mary, wife of Sir John Bankes, Lord Chief Justice of the Common Plea and Privy Councillor to Charles I, showed remarkable coolness and defiance when defending her besieged home. In 1641, Sir John was summoned by the king to attend him in York and left his wife Mary and their children (four sons and six daughters) at his newly acquired home – Corfe Castle. For centuries this castle, set in the isle of Purbeck, in Dorset, had been a royal residence. Strategically built on top of a hill, it had a clear view of the surrounding countryside. The steepness of the hill and the massively thick walls made the castle one of the most impregnable fortresses in the country.

Lady Mary prudently took shelter from the strife of the Civil War in this magnificent structure, laying in a good supply of food. Life was comparatively peaceful until May 1643 when, after the fall of Dorchester, Lyme, Weymouth, Wareham and Poole, the commissioners of the last-named town sent forty seamen to collect – or rather to confiscate – four small cannons from the castle.

These cannons were the castle's only means of defence but the commissioners hoped that Lady Mary would be intimidated by a show of force. However, they had misjudged their opponent. The intrepid Lady Bankes called upon the only five men left in the castle, who, together with her maidservants, mounted the cannons on to their carriages, loaded one of them and fired it. The astounded sailors decided that discretion was the better part of valour and returned post-haste to Poole, empty handed.

When they had gone, Lady Mary summoned help locally and many of her tenants and friends came to the castle, bringing with them about fifty assorted guns. The commissioners now resorted to threatening letters, vowing to set fire to her tenants' houses and to send a large force to reduce the castle. A proclamation was issued in Wareham, stating that any trader sending provisions to the castle or selling goods to any of Lady Bankes's associates would be severely punished. As her provisions were running low, Lady Mary diplomatically started to negotiate with the commissioners, offering to relinquish the cannons in return for supplies. Thinking that she was giving up the struggle, the Roundheads guarding the castle relaxed their vigilance, and while she bargained with them, supplies of food, cattle, gunpowder and other vital necessities were surreptitiously brought into the fortress. She also managed to get a message through to Prince Rupert, Charles I's nephew, and the Marquis of Hertford, who were advancing on Blandford, asking for assistance. In answer to her request they sent eighty men, under the command of Captain Robert Lawrence, to her aid.

On 23 June 1643, Sir William Earle and between 500 and 600 Parliamentarians took over the small town of Corfe, burning some of the houses. They brought with them various artillery pieces and began to bombard the castle. The Roundheads had all been forced to swear an oath 'that if they found the defendants obstinate not to yield, they would maintain the siege to victory and then deny any quarter unto all, killing without mercy, men, women and children'. Sir William could not have had much faith in his soldiers' loyalty because he bribed them with hopes of '... rich booty and the like; so during the siege they used all base unworthy means to corrupt the defendants to betray the castle unto their hands; the better sort they endeavour to corrupt with bribes, to the rest they offer double pay and the whole plunder of the castle.'

To make access to the walls easier, they developed two siege machines which were named the Sowe and the Boare. The great Sowe, 33 ft long and 9 ft wide, was made of solid oak logs bound together with iron hoops. This was set on four wheels and 'had cros beames within to worck with there levars, to forse har along as thaie plesed to guide har'. The top timbers were covered with 'two rowes of hides and two rowes of sheepe skinnes; soe that noe musket bullet or steele arrow could pierce it, of which triell was often made'. This war machine proved pretty useless as the marksmen on the castle walls fired at the only visible parts of the attackers – their legs – so accurately 'that nine ran away, as well as their broken and battered legs would give them leave, and of the two which knew neither how to run away nor well to stay, for feare, one was slaine'. The Boare was of similar design, but smaller and more manoeuvrable than the Sowe, but proved equally useless.

After several more assaults had been repelled by the valiant little garrison, Sir William Earle resorted to giving his men strong drink in order to bolster their flagging spirits. He now divided his forces into two groups, one to assault the middle ward which was defended by Captain Lawrence and most of the soldiers, the other to attack the upper ward which was defended by Lady Bankes, some of her daughters, maids and five soldiers. The defenders heaved stones and hot embers over the walls and 'repelled the rebels and kept them from climbing the ladders'. During this battle a hundred of Sir William's men were either killed or wounded; and hearing that the king's army was heading in his direction, he hastily withdrew his men, leaving behind artillery, ammunition and horses, all of which were removed into the castle. After six weeks of siege, Corfe Castle was left in peace.

This peace lasted for nearly two years although Lady Bankes remained steadfast to the Royalist cause. In December 1644, Sir John

Bankes died and in the following spring of 1645 the Parliamentary forces renewed their efforts to subdue the castle. Corfe was now the only garrison between Exeter and London – and one of the last in England – still holding out for the king. On 17 May the following instructions were sent to Sir A. A. Cooper for the blockade of Corfe Castle.

'At the Committee of Lords and Commons for the safety of the Associated Western Counties – Instructions for Sir A. Cooper Bart – You are desired forthwith to repair to the Isle of Purbeck, and to draw together as speedily as may be, out of the garrisons of Poole, Wareham, Lulworth and Weymouth, such numbers of foot and horse as are sufficient to block up Corfe Castle. And the Governors of the several garrisons aforesaid are hereby desired to give you all the furtherance and assistance they are able in this design, which is of such great consequence to the country. You shall have power to dispose of such moneys as we have given order to Mr Henry Bridges to receive, in such manner as shall be conducible to the carrying on of this service. You shall have power, if either of the commanders or soldiers are willing to render the Castle on composition, that then you shall accept of it on such reasonable conditions for their person and estates as in your discretion shall be thought fit. Lastly, you are authorised to do and execute all things else that in your judgement you shall think necessary for the carrying on all this design; and for the better encouragement both of officers and soldiers herein, you are to let them know they shall each of them have a fortnight pay for their reward.

> Anth. Nicholl. Denzill Holles.
> Denis Bond. Tho. Earle.'

So the second siege began and for forty-eight days, for the loss of only eleven men, Lady Mary and her gallant band defied all the assaults and bombardments that the Parliamentary forces could throw at them. Then an officer (whom historians have kept anonymous), bored with the siege and with the Royalist cause, while pretending to take in provisions under cover of darkness, treacherously let fifty enemy soldiers into the castle. The betrayed garrison, realising that further resistance was useless, gave themselves up. Lady Bankes and her children, having been deprived of all their belongings, were allowed to leave unmolested. She lived to see the king, whom she had supported so loyally for so long, restored to his throne.

Lady Mary died in April 1661 and was interred in Ruislip Church, Middlesex. The inscription on her tomb, dedicated by her son and heir, Sir Ralph Bankes, read as follows:

> 'The Lady Mary Bankes, the only daughter of Rafe Hawtrey, of Ruislip in the county of Middx, Esquire, the wife and widow of Sir John Bankes, Knight, late Lord Chief Justice of his Majesty's Court of Common Pleas, and of the Privy Council to his late Majesty King Charles I of blessed memory; who, having had the honour to have bourne, with a constancy and courage above her sex, a noble proportion of the late calamity, and the happiness to have outlived them so far as to have seen the restitution of the government, with great peace of mind laid down her most desired life the 19th day of April 1661, Sir Ralph Bankes, her son and heir, hath dictated this. She left four sonnes, first Sir Ralph; second Jerome; third Charles; fourth William (since died without issue) and six daughters.'

Cromwell gave orders for Corfe Castle to be undermined and blown up with gunpowder. So this magnificent old building was reduced to a heap of huge chunks of stone which still occupy the site as a permanent monument to Lady Mary and her gallant stand. It is now looked after by the National Trust.

Charlotte Stanley, Countess of Derby

Charlotte Stanley was born at Thouars in France in December 1599. She was the second child, the eldest daughter, of Claude de la Tremoïlle, Duc de Thouars, and his wife Charlotte, daughter of William the Silent, Prince of Orange. Her father died when she was five and she spent her early years at Thouars, with occasional visits to her relations in the Hague.

In 1625 the family came to England – her mother was now in the household of Henrietta Maria, queen to Charles I. During the visit a marriage was arranged between Charlotte and Lord James Strange, who afterwards became the 7th Earl of Derby. They were married on 26 June 1626, had nine children, and for sixteen years lived peacefully and happily together at their homes at Knowsley and Lathom House in Lancashire.

At the outbreak of the Civil War, Lord Strange joined the king, leaving Lady Strange, their children and retainers, at Lathom House. But Lancashire was predominantly in favour of the Parliamentarians and by May 1645, at which time Lord and Lady Strange had become Earl and Countess of Derby, Lathom House was the only place left in the county that was loyal to the king. No attempts were made to reduce the house until February of the following year when Sir William Fairfax and his troops, who were encamped between Bolton and Wigan, began their siege of Lathom.

The house had a garrison of 300 men with six captains and six lieutenants, all under the direct orders of the countess. After a week of protracted negotiations, she totally rejected any idea of surrender, saying that she and her children would rather die at home. There followed sporadic sorties on 17, 18, 19 and 20 March, when the countess managed to get a message through the enemy lines to Prince Rupert and her husband. On 10 April the Roundheads opened their bombardment with a large mortar, which all but finished the defence before it began. However, in a brilliant sally, a small force from Lathom captured the mortar. This successful coup gave fresh encouragement to the defenders, who were further heartened by the news that Prince Rupert was approaching Bolton, which he stormed on 28 May. He sent the countess two banners that he had captured from the force which had been bombarding Lathom.

With their defeat at the battle of Marston Moor on 2 July, the Royalist cause in Lancashire was at its lowest ebb, and by the end of the month Lathom was once again under siege. After several days, in a daring dash by night, the earl managed to rescue the countess and their children and take them to the Isle of Man, before Lathom House surrendered on 8 December. The countess and her children remained on the island until her husband was executed in 1651, and soon afterwards the governor, William Christian, surrendered the isle to the Parliamentarians. The countess and her children then travelled to Knowsley, their other property, where they remained until the Restoration. She died at Knowsley in March 1644 and was buried in Ormskirk church next to her husband.

24

Lady Blanche Arundel

Our third Civil War heroine is Lady Blanche Arundel, daughter of Edward and Elizabeth, Earl and Countess of Worcester. She married Thomas, 2nd Lord Arundel, of Wardour Castle. While her husband was at Oxford with the king, Sir Edward Hungerford and Colonel Strode, with a force of 1300 men, laid siege to the castle. Although she only had twenty-five men and some servants to defend it, she replied to a summons to surrender that 'she had command from her Lord to keep it and she would obey his command'.

The siege guns bombarded the castle from morning till night. Lady Arundel and her maidservants loaded muskets, and even fired them for the garrison, who were all very tired from lack of sleep. Despite this spirited, daring and gallant defence, two mines were placed under the castle, and their explosion brought resistance to an end. Lady Arundel and all the defenders, surprisingly, were allowed to go free. Although the Roundheads had promised not to plunder the castle, they proceeded to burn buildings, slaughter animals, uproot gardens, and loot or destroy all the treasures, including many pictures and about 100,000 books.

Having 'not a bed to lie on, nor means to provide herself with a house or furniture', Lady Blanche went to Salisbury where she was given lodgings by Lord Hertford. She died at Winchester in October 1649 and was buried beside her husband at Tisbury.

Kenau Hasselaar, defender of Haarlem

In 1555 the ailing Charles V, Holy Roman Emperor, handed over power to his only legitimate son Philip. During his reign Charles had built the empire into an immense, sprawling domain, which included not only Spain and its colonies of the New World but also many parts of Europe. One of the jewels of his empire was the prosperous Netherlands, and Charles, who had been born and brought up there, always retained a soft spot for his homeland. Nevertheless, he was concerned at the spread of Protestantism, which had found fertile ground in the Dutch cities and towns, well known for their tolerance. Charles was a devout Catholic and was quite prepared to take the required steps against heretics – burning, racking, drowning and all the other hideous obscenities of the Inquisition.

Apart from one major purge, however, he generally kept the Inquisitors away from the Netherlands, presumably believing that a live tax-paying

Protestant was infinitely better than a dead heretic. On the whole, therefore, he was liked and respected by his hard-working, hard-headed and prosperous Dutch subjects.

His son Philip II was a very different kettle of fish. A fanatical Catholic, he was determined to eradicate Protestantism and to tax the Dutch out of existence. Unlike his father, Philip had no love for the Netherlands and once he had returned to Spain after the death of his wife, Mary of England, he never visited the northern parts of his kingdom again. The continuing spread of heresy and the lack of co-operation from his Dutch subjects led him to send, in 1567, the Duke of Alva and a well-equipped army of 10,000 to pacify the area. The Dutch endured his policy of ruthless butchery for a short time but were soon in open revolt.

In all the many battles waged by the Netherlanders against the Spaniards, the Dutch women displayed as much courage and defiance as their men, fighting alongside them in defence of their homes, families and new religion. They also faced the same terrible punishments, with rape an additional hazard. One of these heroines gained a place in her country's history during the siege of Haarlem in 1573.

Haarlem, some twelve miles from Amsterdam, with its step-gabled houses and warren-like maze of narrow alleys, was one of the most important cities in the Netherlands and one which the Spaniards were determined to capture at any price. In December 1572, a force of 12,000 men, under the command of Frederic of Toledo, was sent to besiege the city.

Kenau Simons Hasselaar was not a young girl but a mature woman in her fifties when the Spanish army laid siege to Haarlem. She raised a force of 300 women and girls to fight in defence of the city walls. She was always to be seen at the head of her corps of fighters, pressing forward to attack the enemy, helping to repair walls or build new defences. She helped the wounded, assisted with the guns, gave encouragement to all who showed signs of flagging, loaded muskets, brought water and seemed to be everywhere at once. Even the Spanish troops could not help but admire the courage and resourcefulness of this redoubtable woman.

For seven months the people of Haarlem resisted all that Don Frederic's army could throw at them, even though he had originally boasted that he would take the city in seven days. It was very difficult to cut off the town completely (and thus starve the population), as there was still a line of communications across Lake Haarlem. Fresh troops and provisions were brought into the town across the lake from Sasenheim, by the fleet of the insurgent Sea Beggars. Eventually the Spaniards had to transport their Zuider Zee fleet to Lake Haarlem, and it was not until the end of May 1573 that the Beggar fleet on the lake was finally crushed. The siege of the city was now watertight. Relief was attempted overland but this was thwarted in a series of engagements.

Haarlem was now doomed and the following month surrendered on the promise of fair and lenient treatment. By the standards of the day, Don Frederic was a model of moderation and spared many lives, including that of Kenau Hasselaar. Nevertheless, all the surviving soldiers were executed – five executioners kept up their grisly work for several days, until their arms were too tired to lift their swords. Those who remained to be killed were tied together, back to back, and were thrown into the River Spaarne to drown. The Beggar governor of Haarlem, Jonkheer Wigbold van Ripperda, was among those beheaded. In all about 2300 people were murdered by the Spaniards.

Kenau is still much revered in Haarlem and throughout Holland, and one of the ships launched by the government shipyards each year used to be named in her honour.

CHAPTER 3

The Visionaries

Of all the women who have claimed to be guided by visions, taking up arms as a result of receiving divine instructions to do so, by far the most famous is the legendary Joan of Arc. She was a formidable opponent, not so much by reason of her youth and beauty (indeed, opinions vary on the latter attribute), nor her military prowess, but because the ignorant, superstitious English soldiers feared her to be a sorceress with supernatural powers.

The only other woman warrior to come anywhere near to St Joan in displaying courage likewise inspired by her heavenly voices, was Agustina, the young maid of Saragossa, whose example during the siege of her city lifted the hearts and fired the determination of her Spanish compatriots.

The third heroine in this category – Louise Michel, known as the Red Virgin – was a French socialist revolutionary from the Paris Commune. Although her fervour was rooted in political conviction rather than religious faith, she was just as fanatically motivated as the two earlier visionaries, risking danger for her beliefs and fighting with comparable bravery.

Joan of Arc

Historians have long argued about the origins of Joan of Arc, known as La Pucelle. Some maintain that she was the love child of Queen Isabel and the Duke of Orléans, others that she was of peasant stock. After reading many books on the subject we have plumped for the latter theory, but as Régine Pernoud points out: 'Not all is clear about Joan and the historian must be the first to recognise it.... She will always leave us with unanswered questions.'

Joan was born in the small village of Domremy, situated between Champagne and Lorraine. Described as a strapping girl with a short neck and a birthmark behind her right ear, she seems to have had an uneventful and normal childhood but did spend long hours in church and was extremely devout. At thirteen she began to hear voices, stating: 'This voice I heard about midday, in summertime, in my father's garden ... it came from the direction of the church.' At first her voices merely told her to be good and faithful but later they instructed her to go and fight like a man, against the English and Burgundian armies, in the service of the Dauphin.

The Hundred Years War, which began in 1337 when Edward III claimed recognition as sovereign of France, lasted until 1453 when, after over 300 years of English rule, Normandy was lost. During this period England, although a comparatively small and poor country, had repeatedly raided France on the pretext that English kings had a legitimate claim to the French throne.

The France of that era was not the united country we know today, but a collection of separate lands owing allegiance to Burgundy, Germany, England and the Dauphin. The English army had won some spectacular battles – Crécy, Poitiers and Agincourt among them – and was considered to be almost invincible; nearly the whole of northern France was occupied by the Anglo-Burgundian allied armies. The crown of France was still in dispute in 1427, between the Dauphin Charles VII (son and heir of Charles VI of France) and Henry VI, king of England (son of the brilliant but short-lived Henry V). The Dauphin had come to the throne five years earlier, but because Reims, the traditional place for the coronation of French kings, was in English hands, he had not yet been crowned.

In 1428 the voices ordered Joan to go to the Dauphin and tell him that she would lead him to victory at Orléans. They were so insistent that she prevailed upon her mother's cousin to accompany her to Vaucouleurs, the nearest garrison loyal to the Dauphin, and to seek permission to visit him. The captain to whom she made the request thought that the sixteen-year-old girl was mad and sent her packing. The following year she managed to convince Captain Robert de Baudricourt of her sincerity and he consented to her visiting the Dauphin at Chinon, even providing her with a small escort on the road to protect her from bandits.

Although Charles himself was impressed by her and convinced that she was telling the truth, he nevertheless insisted that she was questioned by churchmen to ensure that the girl who called herself La Pucelle – the Maid – was not a heretic. He had her physically examined to make quite certain that she was a virgin and not 'been sent by the devil for his evil purposes'. All agreed that Joan should be allowed to do as her voices urged, in the best interests of France.

The city of Orléans, which had been under siege for more than six months, was to be her main objective. Joan, dressed in full armour, with her hair cut short, rode with the Duke of Alençon at the head of the army. She first sent a letter to the Duke of Bedford, declaring: 'Jesus Maria, King of England – and you Duke of Bedford calling yourself Regent of France – deliver up to the Maid sent by God, the King of Heaven, the keys to all the good towns which you have taken and violated in France.' She then set off for Orléans with the force of 4000 men that Charles had raised at Blois.

The voices had told her to attack from the north towards the St Pouvair area but Alençon and Le Hire ignored her suggestions, keeping to the other side of the river, which was not so heavily fortified. Under cover of a diversion they managed to get some much needed supplies into the beleaguered city. It was a hard-fought battle but gradually the French army gained ground. Joan was completely fearless, riding at the head of the troops in full view of the enemy, shouting encouragement and fighting valiantly. She was wounded by an arrow which pierced her shoulder, but was back in the fray as soon as it had been dressed. With one final ferocious attack, against the fort of Tourelles, the French overcame the English and forced their retreat.

Joan then urged the Dauphin to push on for Reims for his coronation, but Charles hesitated. With the backing of the Duke of Alençon, now lieutenant general of the French army, she finally persuaded Charles to continue to push the English out of the other towns along the Loire. Together they led the French army to victory in a series of battles at Jargeau, Meung and Beaugency. Then, on 18 June 1429, the two armies came face to face at Patay. The ensuing battle was the greatest victory so far for the French. The English army, hitherto invincible, was completely routed.

Instead of pressing home their advantage and attacking Paris – as Joan and the French commanders begged him to do – the vacillating Charles, now completely under the influence of his favourite Georges de La Trémoïlle, refused, preferring instead to visit the rescued towns along the Loire. But at last Joan persuaded the Dauphin to set off for Rheims. Arriving at Troyes, Joan sent a message to the citizens promising them freedom if they would submit. They refused, saying that they would remain loyal to the English, but as soon as the French began to attack, Troyes surrendered. The army marched to Chalons, which gave up its keys, and finally the gates of Rheims were opened to them and Charles was crowned the following day.

Three days later, 20 July, he left Reims to make a triumphal tour of Champagne, but on 14 August the English and French armies again came face to face at Patay. This time there was no major battle, merely a few minor skirmishes. Beauvais and Senlis and other towns north of Paris then surrendered to Charles and Joan.

The French were now on the outskirts of Paris itself. The inhabitants were busy organising their defences when Joan, standing on a vantage point, called on them to surrender to the King of France. An English chronicler related that Charles:

'lodged his armie at Monmartir nere adjoining and lying to the Citie of Paris. And from thence sent John, Duke of Alençon, and his sorceress Ioan ... with three thousand light horsemen, to get again the Citie of Paris; but the Englishe captaynes, every one kepying hys warde and place assigned so manfully and fiercely with noble courage defended themselves, their walles and towers, with the assistance of the Parisians, that they rebutted and drave away the Frenchmen....'

A French chronicler stated that Joan and the army attacked St Honoré at about ten in the morning, that fighting continued for about five hours and that during the course of the battle '... Joan the Maid was gravely wounded and lay in a trench behind an ass until the hour of vespers when Guichard de Tienbronne and others went to search for her, but several of them too were wounded...'

This was not the result that the confident French army had expected and Charles immediately got cold feet. Using Joan's wound as an excuse, he finished the campaign and disbanded the army. Alençon and the other commanders returned to their estates but Joan remained with the king. Her enemies at court, however, were growing tired of her and plotted, with the king's connivance, to get rid of her. She was impatient to mount another attack on Paris, so in order to keep her quiet she was given a small force.

Her repeated requests for additional ammunition and supplies were ignored. During a skirmish she was captured by the Burgundians and handed over to the English.

She was imprisoned in Bouvreuil Castle – then occupied by the Earl of Warwick, the English commander at Rouen, and her trial began in March 1431. She had seventy charges to answer, based mainly on the premise that her behaviour had been 'blasphemous, immodest and presumptuous'. The hearing was before a church court, in order to avoid embarrassment to the English who could not afford to try such a popular figure.

After steadfastly refusing to sign a prepared document admitting the charges, Joan suddenly wavered, and frightened by the thought of burning at the stake, she signed the document. A week later she realised what she had done and renounced her confession. She was immediately sentenced to death and was publicly burned at the stake on 30 May 1431. After her death her almost mystical reputation grew apace and her martyrdom served to enhance it. She was canonised in May 1920 and a month later the French Parliament decreed that a national feast day would be held in her honour each year on the second Sunday in May. La Pucelle had indeed triumphed over all her enemies.

Agustina, the Maid of Saragossa

In 1808 the Spanish people, angered by Napoleon's domination of their country, grew restless. The trouble was brought to a head when he deposed the Spanish royal family and placed his brother Joseph Bonaparte on the throne. Saragossa, capital of Aragon, was among the first cities to show signs of discontent and one of its leading citizens became involved with the burgeoning revolution.

Don José Palafox y Melzi was born in Saragossa in 1775. He was the youngest son of an aristocratic family, one of the oldest in Aragon, and in 1808 was promoted to brigadier of the Royal Bodyguard. In May of the same year, the citizens of Saragossa expressed their wrath at the French intervention in their daily lives and the deposition of the Spanish King Charles IV and broke out into open revolt.

The siege of Saragossa by a strong division of the French army under Marshal Lefebvre began in June 1808 and was to test the heroism of the whole population of the beleaguered town. The 60,000 inhabitants, with only ten dilapidated guns and 220 regular soldiers, faced the might of France. The town was enclosed by a badly constructed, discontinuous wall, about twelve feet high and three feet wide, that hardly formed the ideal barricade. It was bordered on the northern side by the River Ebro and there were five gates into the town, called the Sancho, Portillo, Carmen, Santa Engracia and Quemada.

Preparations for the defence were still incomplete when the French first came into view. Armed with every available weapon, the civilians hastily occupied every vantage point – windows, balconies, walls and rooftops. In the intense heat of high summer, the French advanced to within about half a mile of the walls, where Lefebvre halted his army to give them final orders for the attack. Thinking that there was little likelihood of strong opposition, he planned to advance in three columns – to the Portillo gate in the west, the Carmen gate in the centre and the Santa Engracia gate in the east.

As the first shots were fired, the streets leading to the walls were filled with excited and enthusiastic crowds carrying guns, ammunition, provisions and water. As the French attack began, the townspeople swarmed to defend the gates. Alcaide Ibieca, who was present at the time, wrote:

'It is impossible to give an idea of every detail of that scene; what is certain is that the Calle de la Puerta del Carmen was covered with people, the major part of them armed, that in the mass there were some women, old men and boys, that now a platoon would detach itself to go towards the Plaza de Portillo, now towards Puerta de Santa Engracia, that some were carrying the wounded on their shoulders, that others, especially the womenfolk, were rushing towards the cannon to give drink to the gunners, that spirit reigned in every countenance, that they looked calmly or even enviously at the inanimate or dead citizens, that priests and monks came to give them their last comfort and that there were quarrels because the defenders would not let them go to the gate.'

The central column attacking the Carmen gate met determined resistance – the defenders being aided by colleagues from the Santa Engracia.

Lefebvre, realising that the latter gate was sparsely protected, sent his cavalry who burst through and swept into the main plaza. As they rode wildly round the square, the civilians from surrounding houses attacked them with knives, scissors, hatchets, sickles and spades – and anything else that would serve as a weapon. Few of the cavalry survived and those who did beat a hasty retreat.

News of the battle quickly spread throughout Spain as it was the first victory against the oppressors. This brought many more volunteers to Saragossa, together with military reinforcements from Madrid and Barcelona. The Junta issued a statement: 'Aragonese, your heroic valour in the defence of the justest cause which history can present was made manifest yesterday by the triumph we won. The 15th June will make your exploits known to all Europe and history will record them with admiration.' But the main siege was yet to come.

At one o'clock on the morning of 30 June the French began their preliminary bombardment. The Alcaide Ibieca, again an eyewitness, wrote:

'It is impossible to describe the haste with which we worked and the variety of scenes which took place. As shooting died down in one spot it broke out with even greater violence in another. Soldiers and civilians came running through the streets towards the batteries, bringing carts and munitions; some others went to Lazan to complain of the disorder and ask for reinforcements. The citizens were awed by the continuous crash of bombs and grenades. The horror of it all was accentuated by the tolling of the great bell and the quivering of the ground under each explosion. It seemed that there was not one single place in which one might hide from death.'

On 2 July, after twenty-seven hours of continuous bombardment, the guns fell silent and the French infantry stormed the gates. After assaults on the Sancho, Carmen and Santa Engracia gates had been repulsed, the French concentrated on the Portillo gate where over fifty of the gallant defenders were killed or wounded. Through the gap the few remaining stalwarts could see the faces of the French infantry, still grimly moving forwards with their bayonets fixed.

It was in this desperate situation that our heroine arrived on the scene. Agustina Domonech, an attractive young girl, was taking water to the hot and weary soldiers when she saw the gap in the defences. Dropping her pail, she snatched up a burning brand from the hand of a dying soldier and set off, at point blank range, a twenty-six pounder gun. The effect at such close quarters was devastating and enough to deter the advancing French infantry. Leaping on to the damaged ramparts, Agustina called to the people in the vicinity, exhorting them to 'Death or Victory'. Inspired by the sight of this young girl with eyes ablaze and hair streaming behind her, the weary die-hards renewed their efforts and rushed into the breach, blazing away at the French. Agustina's action had saved the day and, as her fame quickly spread throughout Spain, she became the symbol of her beleaguered country. Goya was inspired to include her in his series of etchings called *The Disasters of War*, picturing her – a slight figure beside a huge cannon – under the title 'Que Valor'.

The fighting continued and Agustina daily risked her life assisting the wounded, carrying ammunition and helping to defend the north- western gate. For eleven days and nights the war to the death continued, with the Spaniards stubbornly defending every street and house. At last the French, thoroughly exhausted, retired to Pamplona. Their casualties were 200 dead and 300 wounded. Palafox issued this statement: 'Saragossans, this day will be immortal in the annals of your history, and all nations will enviously admire your heroism.'

Their ordeal, of course, was not yet over, but fortunately, during the respite, reinforcements reached Saragossa. The dense olive groves near to the walls, which had served as cover for the advancing French, were cut down and the wood used to bolster up damaged walls and repair barricades and batteries. The French were now determined to starve the citizens into submission by means of a complete blockade. They dug trenches towards the gate and brought up heavy siege guns ready to breach the walls. Before the attack commenced, General Verdier once again demanded surrender. On 30 July, Palafox addressed his compatriots:

'Aragonese, for the third time General Verdier has summoned
me to surrender the city and my reply has been the same as
previously. From tomorrow, one hundred siege guns with which

the French think to intimidate us, will fire without interruption upon the city. But what are a hundred guns to us?'

The renewed bombardment was heavier than ever. Once again Agustina and the women of Saragossa formed themselves into groups to tend the wounded and to carry water, food and ammunition to the soldiers. Cannon and mortar shells rained down on the inhabitants until they were shattered in mind and body. During one particularly bad attack, while Agustina was assisting a battery, a shell exploded, killing most of the soldiers. As they fell on top of her she was pinned to the ground and almost suffocated under the weight of bodies before being rescued. But she vowed never to leave the gun while she was alive. The fighting was now from house to house and again the call came for surrender. The reply the defenders sent back was the famous 'War even to the knife'.

Agustina and a small group managed to capture fifteen French grenadiers but they were rescued by some of their comrades and Agustina was taken prisoner. A sergeant was holding her by the throat but released her on the entrance of his captain, who later wrote:

'Pale with anger and surprise, motionless but proud, Agustina summoned me in a lofty tone which, however, was tinged with a certain sweetness. "Do what you will," she said, "but por Dios, if you have any heart, do not deliver the heroine of the Portillo, who is under the protection of our Lady of the Pillar, to the brutality of your soldiers.... My honour and my life are both in peril – let it only be my life." She stood very close to me. Her serene and smiling face suddenly lit up and you would have said she was praying. "Oh Virgin of the Pillar,"she cried as she flung her arms around my neck and kissed me, "Adieu." All of a sudden she jumped nimbly through the window and disappeared into the dusk.... We rushed out ... in pursuit of the fugitive but it was impossible for us to find any trace of her.'

The two sieges of Saragossa had finally ended. When the French eventually broke into the city they had to fight for a further twenty-four days from house to house, street to street and in every church, monastery and public building. Saragossa was a smouldering, shattered city – over a third was in complete ruins and every building was in some way damaged. Worst of all, more than 54,000 civilians and soldiers had died, not just from the shelling and bombardments, but also of disease.

Years later Lord Byron met Agustina in a park in Seville, wearing a skirt but with an artilleryman's jacket (a reward for heroism in addition to being decorated with medals). He was inspired to include a passage dedicated to Agustina in his *Childe Harold's Pilgrimage:*

> 'Ye who shall marvel when you hear the tale
>   Oh! had you known her in her softer hour,
> Mark'd her black eye that mocks her coal-black veil,
>   Heard her light lively tones in lady's bower,
> Seen her long locks that foil the painter's power,
>   Her fairy form, with more than female grace;
> Scarce would you deem that Saragossa's tower
>   Beheld her smile in danger's Gorgon face,
> Thins the closed ranks, and leads in glory's fearful chase.'

Agustina lived to the age of sixty-nine and died in Cuesta in July 1857. She was buried 'with all honours due to her', in the Portillo church.

Louise Michel, the Red Virgin

One of the most tempestuous and certainly the most famous of the female Communards, who earned herself the nickname of the Red Virgin, was Louise Clemence Michel. She was born in a castle of the Haute-Marne in 1830, the illegitimate daughter of the son of the house and his chambermaid. With assistance from her father's parents, she was brought up by her mother, a Catholic and an avid reader of Rousseau and Voltaire. Louise became an ardent admirer of Victor Hugo and at one time carried on a lengthy correspondence with him, dedicating some of her own poetry to him.

Louise became a school teacher, but with her revolutionary ideas was soon in trouble, and at the age of twenty-four she moved to Paris, reading science and natural history at night school. By 1853 she had already established a reputation of being an anti-Bonapartist 'red'. As one of the most active and fanatical members of the 18th *arrondissement* (Montmartre) vigilance committee, she spent many hours in Blanqi's club 'La Patrie en Danger' and wrote later that there she had spent 'the finest hours of the siege ... one was a little more fully alive there, with the joy of feeling oneself in one's element in the midst of the intense struggle for liberty'.

France was now engaged in war with Prussia but with little hope of winning. The citizens of Paris were preparing for the defence of their city and all the public gardens and parks were annexed for agriculture, in order to provide food in case of a protracted siege. *The Illustrated London News* reported:

> 'At the moment the destruction of that beautiful resort of elegance and fashion, the Parc de Boulogne, is contemplated.... There are prodigious herds of cattle and flocks of sheep in the Bois de Boulogne. These animals are allowed not only to graze but also to eat the leaves of the trees doomed to destruction.'

The defeat of Emperor Napoleon III at Sedan in 1870 was followed by the capitulation of the new government, which sought to negotiate an armistice with Prussia. The Parisians were furious and humiliated, and the bitterness increased when the victorious Germans marched through the Arc de Triomphe to the Place de la Concorde. They sensed that they had been betrayed and were aroused to fever pitch. Louise was now a familiar sight stalking about the streets in male uniform, with a rifle (bayonet fixed) slung over her shoulder, giving rousing speeches and demanding money for the installation of National Guard ambulances.

Hearing of the armistice negotiations, a mob of infuriated Parisians, comprising mainly writers, painters, intellectuals, small tradesmen and labourers, led by various extremists and accompanied by Louise, swarmed into the Place de l'Hôtel de Ville. Soldiers of the regular French army were already occupying the town hall and were ready to defend it. A random shot was fired; in the confusion no one knew which side had fired it, and a sharp battle ensued. Louise wrote: 'I could not take my eyes off the pale savage figures who were firing on us, emotionlessly, mechanically, as they would have fired on a pack of wolves. I thought – we will have you one day, you scoundrels....' Driven to a frenzy by the sight of the soldiers aiming at the mob, Louise, shooting to kill, railed at those of her companions who were merely firing at the walls of the town hall. In all about thirty civilians and National Guards were killed.

Louise firmly believed that their next step should be the assassination of the president, Adolf Thiers, who had been so ready to make bargains with the Prussians. (In a peace treaty France agreed to surrender to Germany all of Alsace and most of Lorraine, and also to pay an indemnity of five billion francs.) However, the vigilance committee refused to back her suggestion, deeming it foolhardy. Undismayed, she disguised herself, slipped past the guards at Versailles and brought back a trophy as proof that she had made a successful entry, thus proving that it could be done – but they still remained unresponsive to her suggestions.

The government now committed an even greater blunder by ordering the army into Paris to seize the cannons at Montmartre, held by the National Guard. Learning of these plans from one of their spies, the guard and hundreds of ordinary civilians raced excitedly to the top of Montmartre. Louise wrote: 'I went with my rifle under my coat crying "TREASON"... We expected to die for liberty. It was almost as if we were lifted from the earth.' There was a confrontation and all the women pushed to the front and stood between the army and the National Guard. When the order came for the army to fire on the crowd, the soldiers mutinied.

The Communards then went on a rampage, setting fire to the Hôtel de Ville, the Tuileries Palace, the Palais de Justice, the Préfecture de Police, the Arsenal and many other government buildings. The Place de la Concorde was a complete shambles; blazing houses in the Faubourg St Honoré, Rue Royale and Rue Haussmann added to the chaos. If the Communards had followed up their advantage and pressed on to Versailles, who knows what the outcome might have been? As it was they hesitated and troops from Versailles marched on Paris, beginning the bombardment on 1 May.

Louise was everywhere – making speeches, fighting at the barricades, tending the sick and wounded and organising the women with the Commune ambulances. Some of the most ferocious resistance came from her women's brigade, who fought from barricade to barricade along the Boulevard de Clichy, around the Place Blanche to the Place Pigalle. Then, realising that they were being outflanked, and that their numbers were vastly reduced – the streets of Montmartre were littered with their bodies – Louise moved her brigade to join the men at Belleville. The final battle took place among the tombstones of the Père Lachaise cemetery.

When the collapse came, Louise somehow managed to escape, took refuge with a friend and then made her way home. To her horror she discovered that her mother had been arrested and was being held as hostage, so she immediately gave herself up.

Georges Clemonceau, who was then mayor of Montmartre, wrote: 'They fought like devils, far better than the men; I had the pain of seeing fifty of them shot down, even when they had been surrounded by troops and disarmed. I saw about sixty men shot at the same time.' The Communards in their turn executed sixty-seven hostages, including the Archbishop of Paris.

Louise was marched with the other prisoners to the Satory depot which she described: 'On the floor were snaky, silvery little threads forming currents between veritable lakes, large as anthills, and filled like rivulets with a nacreous swarm. They were lice.' She was not brought to trial until December 1871 although many Communards had been shot without trial in Satory. In an unparalleled bloodbath the government subsequently rounded up and executed 20,000 Parisians. Perhaps unwilling to allow her to become a martyr, it decided to put Louise on trial. She appeared in court in a black veil in mourning for those who had been executed. She admitted every charge whether true or false, acknowledging, however, that she had helped to burn Paris:

'I wanted to oppose the Versailles invaders with a barrier of flames.... Since it appears that every heart that beats for freedom has no right to anything but a slug of lead, I demand my share. If you let me live I shall never cease to cry for vengeance. If you are not cowards, kill me.'

The court refused her offer of martyrdom and sentenced her to transportation to a penal colony in the South Pacific; thousands of others were also sent there.

After serving her nine years' sentence, enduring, at her own insistence, the same treatment as the male prisoners, Louise was repatriated to France – still an ardent activist. She held frequent public political meetings, always attended by capacity crowds. Needless to say, the police followed her everywhere and three years after her return she was again arrested for conspiracy, and gaoled for another three years. On her release she embarked on more public speeches and at one such meeting was shot in the head by a Breton – who obviously did not agree with her politics. She had the bullet removed and when she had recovered, continued her meetings.

But France was getting too dangerous for her and eventually she took refuge in London. Here she met a young art student also with anarchistic leanings – Augustus John – and made a strong impression on him. She enjoyed London and lived a reasonably quiet life there, writing books on the Commune and making the occasional short trip back to France. It was during one of these visits, to Marseilles, in January 1905, that Louise died, aged seventy-four.

There were arguments as to where her funeral should be held and who should be responsible for it. It was finally decided to hold it in Paris. The ceremony brought traffic to a standstill and produced the largest crowd since Victor Hugo's funeral nine years earlier.

CHAPTER 4

The Patriots

P atriotic beliefs have, throughout history, inspired many women who have fought for their country alongside their menfolk. The female partisans in the Soviet Union and Yugoslavia and the other Resistance fighters all over occupied Europe, who fought against the Nazis during the Second World War, are typical examples. These women suffered the most dreadful tortures and indignities when captured and yet tens of thousands of them contributed in some way or other to the fight against their oppressors. Some were parachuted into Europe from England, as members of the Special Operations Executive (SOE). Pearl Witherington landed in central France in 1943 and became a courier for a local agent. When arrested in 1944, Pearl assumed control of a large piece of his territory, her Maquis being responsible for killing over 1000 Germans. Another was Nancy Wake, the New Zealand-born wife of a wealthy French industrialist. She was originally a member of the Maquis, then escaped to England where she joined the SOE. She was trained and returned to France to help train and lead various Maquis groups. She showed great bravery under fire and was awarded the George Medal and many other decorations for her work.

Renée Bordereau, heroine of La Vendée

The Wars of La Vendée was the name applied to the five counter-revolutionary insurrections that took place in western France between 1789 and 1832. The first and most important occurred in the Vendée region in 1793, where there was a general uprising following the introduction of the Conscription Acts in that year. It was a fervently religious and backward area in which there had been little real enthusiasm for the revolution of 1789. The people who were still loyal to the monarchy and the church rose in early March at Cholet and by the middle of the month the whole of the

Vendée was in open revolt. This disturbance coincided with troubles in Lyons, Marseilles and Normandy and created many problems for the revolutionary government. Royalist nobles joined the peasant leaders and the 30,000-strong 'Catholic and Royal Army', which later changed its name to 'La Grande Armée', took the towns of Thousars, Parthenay, Fontenay and Saumur. It was the first army of untrained and virtually unarmed peasants to defeat regular troops and to practise what is now called 'total war', in which everyone in the province – men, women and children – took part. In the few pitched battles of the insurrection the Vendéans did not attempt to emulate the set-piece tactics of trained troops, but threw themselves in a howling mob, from all sides – a manoeuvre known as 'le grand choc'. Normally, though, they fought in open order, making full use of natural cover and camouflage. By mid-June the Grand Army had crossed the River Loire and taken Angers, but had failed to capture the important centre of Nantes. The successful defence of Nantes by the Republicans prevented the peasants uniting Brittany, Normandy and Maine and foiled their plan to march on Paris.

By the autumn, government forces had been reinforced and on 17 October they heavily defeated the main Vendée army at Cholet. Most of the peasants and soldiers, too, fled north across the Loire, leaving only a token force to continue the fight. From then on they had little success, losing battle after battle, one of the most bloody being that of Le Mans where 15,000 rebels were killed, including many prisoners who were butchered by their captors. Having defeated the main insurgent army, Republican soldiers now rampaged through the Vendée, killing and looting without mercy. Among those murdered were forty-two members of the Bordereau family, including the father of a young woman named Renée.

Renée Bordereau was born in June 1766 in the village of Soulaine, near Angers, of 'poor but honest stock'. She became the most famous of the female soldiers of the insurrection, and was commonly known as 'L'Angevin' after her birthplace.

Having witnessed her father's murder, she was filled with a burning hatred and vowed that she would be avenged against the Republic. She bought a light musket, with double sights, secretly learned how to load, prime, aim and fire it, and practised until she was a very good shot. She also taught herself military drill and when she reckoned that she was proficient enough to pass muster, she put on male clothing and volunteered for the Royalist forces. She joined a corps commanded by a Monsieur 'Coeur de Roi'. (We have been unable to discover the true identity of this nobleman but it is suggested that it could have been the Comte de la Rochejaquelin, who became Generalissimo of the Grand Army at the age of twenty-two. He and his sister-in-law petitioned on Renée's behalf, years later, for an increase in her pension.)

During the years of sporadic insurrections she took part in over 200 battles or skirmishes, usually fighting on horseback but occasionally, in order to get to grips with the enemy, on foot. She was always in the thick of the fray, volunteering for the most difficult and dangerous missions, and never leaving the battlefield unless compelled to do so. No one ever suspected that she was a woman and she became a byword for courage among the peasants all over France. Having sworn vengeance for her father's death, she would not give up fighting until the legitimate king had been restored to his throne.

Her prowess and status were such that when Napoleon finally subdued the Vendée and executed the ringleaders, he deliberately did not include L'Angevin in the general amnesty granted to the peasants, but instead put a price on her head. This inevitably led to Renée being betrayed and at this time she was also discovered to be a woman; nevertheless she spent the next three years, in chains, in Angers prison. She was then taken to Mont St Michel for two more years of imprisonment, where she was chained in a 'loathsome dungeon and fed on nothing but the coarsest bread and had to collect rainwater in a rusty basin'. Despite these hardships Renée never faltered in her loyalty to the Royalist cause and she was released when the monarchy was restored, and later was presented to Louis XVIII.

Renée's main difficulty, when released from prison, was to get the authorities to pay her a proper military pension; her documents contain many appeals, written both by herself and various influential friends, to the bureaucrats in Paris, asking for more money. Initially she had approached the king in August 1814, explaining that she was asking for a pension in view of her service in the Vendée insurrections. She informed him that she and her family had always been devoted subjects of the Bourbons, that she had been wounded three times and was one of the few peasants still alive who had fought in these battles. She had received a bullet in the cheek under the left eye, at Lucon, her father had been murdered in front of her and nearly all her relations had been killed by the Republicans. Now without a home, she had to live with a relative but had been ousted by one of the king's enemies and put into prison. Moreover, her brother had died of his wounds, leaving two young daughters whom she was now trying to support. She ended with an impassioned plea to the king, saying he was 'her only hope of succour and for whom she was ready to lay down her own life'. This stirring appeal from such a loyal subject clearly moved Louis who granted her a pension of 200 francs.

Unfortunately, Renée found it impossible to keep herself and her adopted family on that sum and she had to write again – to the Finance Ministry – requesting more money. She wrote again five months later, repeating the story she had originally given to the king, detailing her wounds, the horses and equipment she had lost in battle, and the indignities her surviving family had suffered. Her new appeals eventually brought her a further 300 francs and the following year fresh requests on her behalf from such nobleman as the Duc de la Châtre and the Comte de Bournville produced an additional 150 francs. Thus by the end of eighteen months she had received 800 francs in all, the last payment being made on the understanding that she would stop making a nuisance of herself, depart from Paris and return home.

Although she did leave Paris, Renée was made of sterner stuff than the bureaucrats had anticipated and she continued to bombard them with a stream of petitions for more money. A doctor's certificate was produced in September 1816, stating that now she was aged forty-nine she was in great pain because of her wounds – experiencing difficulty in moving her jaw from the bullet wound, her neck from a sabre slash and her right leg from another bullet wound. The doctor, impressed by her courage, had offered his services free. This time the mayor of Cholet sent in the petition, explaining that she was now too ill to sign her own name, but he fully supported her claim.

The Ministry of War's reply was as follows:

a.   That the original pension, granted by the king, had been given as a great favour – normally soldiers had to serve nineteen years of uninterrupted service in order to qualify for a pension.

b.   That a soldier of equivalent grade to L'Angevin received a pension of only 150 francs and she already had more than five times that amount.

c.   That a new law (passed in March 1817) had closed the door to such awards so she was very lucky to have received anything at all.

d.   That they could not be held responsible for all that she and her family had lost or had stolen during the insurrection, nor could it influence the size of her pension.

Naturally, a steadfast fighter such as Renée was not put off by such remarks and she went on petitioning until the end of her life. One of the last appeals on her behalf, in May 1819, was made by Madame la Marquise de la Roche-jacquelin, widow of the famous Vendéan leader, but like all the others it fell on deaf ears and the indomitable Renée just faded away.

Heroines of the American Civil War

An incredibly large number of patriotic women served as soldiers on both sides during the American Civil War. It was said, for example, that during the summer of 1864 more than 150 women were known to be serving in the Army of the Potomac, nearly half being disguised as officers' servants. Mary A. Livermore, in her book *My Story of the War* which was published in 1889, reckoned that the figure was very much higher; indeed she put the number of women who actually bore arms and served in the ranks as more than 400.

On the Union side there were women like Bridget Devens, known as 'Michigan Bridget' who went with her husband, a private in the 1st Michigan Cavalry. She served throughout the war, on occasion taking the place of a soldier when he fell and fighting in his stead. Sometimes she rallied the troops when they were retreating, at other times she brought the wounded off the battlefield. Fearless and daring, she was always a good soldier, far better than many of the men. Her love for the army continued after the war when, together with her husband, she joined the regular army and went to a unit stationed out on the plains.

Kady Brownell accompanied the 5th Rhode Island Infantry into war – her husband being an NCO in that regiment. She held the proud position of colour bearer and was both a skilled sharpshooter and an expert swordswoman. She marched with the men and never asked for special treatment. When her husband was badly wounded and discharged as unfit for further service, Kady also obtained her discharge so that she could look after him.

Frances L. Clayton likewise enlisted in the same company as her husband, at St Paul, Minnesota. They fought side by side, through eighteen battles, until he was killed at the battle of Stone River. She then went to the general, told him she was a woman, that she had been wounded three times and taken prisoner once, and that she did not want to go on fighting without her husband. She was immediately discharged.

The amazing Jennie Hidgers, posing as Albert Cashier, fought for four years without detection and even continued when the war was over. It was not until she was sent to a veterans' hospital after a car accident in 1911 that her sex was discovered. The investigation that followed revealed that her comrades had merely thought her stand-offish and difficult to get to know, none of them dreaming that she was a woman.

There were just as many fighting women on the Confederate side. Amy Clarke enlisted with her husband and continued to serve even after he was killed at the battle of Shiloh; not until she was wounded and captured by Union troops was her true sex revealed. Her captors gallantly gave her a dress and, when she was better, set her free and told her to go home. Instead she rejoined to fight for the Southern cause.

Many of these women were the subject of newspaper reports. The following appeared just after the battle of Chattanooga in the *Brooklyn Times*:

'About a twelve month since, when disaster everywhere overtook the Union army and our gallant sons were falling fast under the marvellous sword of rebellion, a young lady, scarce nineteen, from an academy in a sister State, conceived the idea that she was destined by Providence to lead our armies to victory, and our nation through a successful war. It was at first thought by her parents – a highly respectable family – that her mind was weakened simply by reading continual accounts of reverses to our arms, and they treated her as a sick child. This only had the effect of making her more demonstrative and her enthusiastic declaration and apparent sincerity gave her family great anxiety. Doctor B. was consulted, the minister was spoken to, friends advised, family meetings held, interviews with the young lady and her former companions in the academy were frequent but nothing could shake the feeling which possessed her.'

Eventually her family decided to put her in the care of an elderly maiden aunt who lived in Michigan. However, the enterprising and deluded girl escaped from the house, and although her parents employed two detectives to find her, she was not found. In fact, she had joined the drum corps of a Michigan regiment, went through the Kentucky campaigns until she was hit by a Minie ball, and when taken to the surgery tent, to everyone's consternation, her sex was discovered. The surgeon told her that she would not recover from her wound and persuaded her to let him contact her family. It was a sad and brief reunion.

The majority of these daring women were 'entrenched in secrecy and regarded as men'. But one who was recognised to be a woman and acclaimed for her bravery in battle was Annie Etheridge. She had started before the war as a laundress with the 3rd Michigan Regiment – it was normal for a number of soldiers' wives to be allowed with every unit – in peacetime – to act as laundresses, for which they received government rations and some monetary compensation. Even so, they were looked on with mixed feelings, some regarding them as good, honest and industrious, others reckoning that they were more trouble than they were worth, especially in isolated posts such as those of the western border.

When the regiment left Washington to march to the front, all the other laundresses departed for home, leaving Annie as sole representative of her sex. She marched to war with the men. Not that she was pugnacious by nature, quite the opposite; it is recorded that she was 'modest, quiet, industrious and a remarkably attractive girl', and anyone who dared say a word against her would have to fight every soldier in the 3rd Michigan! She was seen by General Phil Kearny during one battle whilst attending the wounded at a front-line dressing station and thereafter he saw to it that she was provided with a horse and saddle. Officially she was employed to cook for the officers' mess, drawing sergeant's pay and wearing three stripes on her black riding habit.

During the battle of Chancellorsville, amid the heaviest fighting, up rode Annie, with canteens full of coffee and a sack of hardtack biscuits. During the heavy bombardment, she never flinched or showed the slightest emotion or fear, and later appeared beside a gun battery whose gun crews had been shot to pieces and were about to withdraw and leave the guns to the enemy. She drew up her horse and yelled: 'That's right boys – now you've got good range, keep it up and you'll soon silence those guns!' The men cheered her and went back to their field pieces, remarking later that not all the officers in the army could have had so much influence with them at that moment as 'that brave little sergeant in skirts'. Her courage did not go unrewarded and one morning, shortly after the battle, she was presented with a special medal for valour by the divisional commander General David Birney, in front of the entire division.

Belle Boyd, 'La Belle Rebelle'

Belle Boyd was born in the peaceful little village of Martinsburg, in the Shenandoah valley of West Virginia, in May 1844. Her family owned the general store and her father also managed a tobacco plantation. The eldest of eight children, she was christened Isabelle, and at the age of eight was sent for her formal education to the Mount Washington Female College in Baltimore. At sixteen, after completing a course in French, classical literature and music, she made her entrée into the social whirl of Washington society. The winter of 1860–1 was to be her only chance to enjoy the gaiety and pleasures of a city which she later likened to Paris in 1789, when 'the elements of a stupendous revolution were yet hidden beneath a tranquil and deceitful surface'.

With the outbreak of the Civil War, Belle returned home to Martinsburg and her family. She was intensely loyal to the Confederate cause and straight away helped to raise funds to arm the soldiers of the locally raised 2nd Virginian Regiment. Her father was among the first to volunteer to join them and the regiment shortly became part of the famous 'Stonewall Brigade'. Their regimental colours were aptly inscribed with the words: 'Our God, our country, our women', and the regiment was soon ordered to Harper's Ferry to protect 'the sacred soil of Virginia from invasion', as Belle put it in her autobiography. It must have been very frustrating for someone of Belle's wayward temperament, to be left at home and do nothing, while the men did all the fighting. She was further incensed when Union troops occupied Martinsburg: 'We could before long hear the rumbling of the guncarriages, and worse than this, the hellish shouts with which the undisciplined soldiers poured into the town.'

The day following the occupation was 4 July – Independence Day. Federal troops tried to force their way into the family home on that particular day, and also brought a Union flag to hoist on the roof. Her mother firmly told the soldiers that 'every member of her household would die before that flag shall be raised over us', and when one of the soldiers made a threatening move towards her, a horrified and furious Belle drew out her pistol (she was always armed after the menfolk had left, in case of 'insult or outrage') and shot him dead. Fortunately, the senior Federal officer in the village decided that she had been quite within her rights to shoot the man, and showed considerable sympathy towards Belle and her family, even providing guards for their house to prevent a similar occurrence.

Belle soon found that she was able to obtain a lot of useful information from seemingly innocent conversations with various admiring Federal officers, and she then sent her gleanings, via a team of messengers, to the Confederates. But this was only the beginning of her career in espionage and she was still very inexperienced. In consequence, she was soon discovered and received a stern reprimand – which did nothing but strengthen her resolve. By the autumn of 1861 she had been officially appointed to the Confederate intelligence service as a courier for Generals Beauregard and Jackson, a perfect job for someone of her abilities as a horsewoman, with an extensive knowledge of the local area. She was also engaged in smuggling much-needed medical supplies across the Potomac River, so it was not unexpected when, early in 1862, she was arrested on suspicion and taken to Baltimore. Another prisoner with the party gave her a small Confederate flag and she arrived at the prison triumphantly waving it above her head. Fortunately, the Federal officers saw the funny side of this display of bravado. For a week she was kept in the Eutaw House, one of the largest and best hotels in Baltimore, and treated with every courtesy and consideration. Then, as the duty officer had received no charge against her, she was released and sent home.

Belle returned to Virginia, living with her aunt at Front Royal, south of Winchester but still in the Shenandoah valley. Soon she had again collected a lot of useful information by talking to the young Union officers in the town. She also did some real spying on a General Shields while he held a council of war in her aunt's drawing room. Belle recalled the incident thus:

'The night before the departure of General Shields, who was about, as he informed us, to "whip" Jackson, a council of war was held in what had formerly been my aunt's drawing room. Immediately above this was a bedchamber containing a closet, through the floor of which I observed a hole had been bored, whether with a view to espionage or not I have never been able to ascertain. It occurred to me, however, that I might turn the discovery to account; and as soon as the council of war had assembled, I stole softly upstairs, and lying down on the floor of the closet, applied my ear to the hole, and found to my great joy, I could distinctly hear the conversation that was passing below.

'The council prolonged their discussion for some hours; but I remained motionless and silent until the proceedings were brought to a conclusion, at one in the morning. As soon as the coast was clear I crossed the courtyard and made my way to my own room, and took down in cypher everything I had heard which seemed to me of importance. I felt that to rouse a servant, or make any disturbance at that hour, would excite the suspicions of the Federals by whom I was surrounded; accordingly I went straight to the stables myself, saddled my horse, and galloped away in the direction of the mountains....'

Twice she was challenged by Federal sentries, but managed to get past them with a false passport she had procured. Once clear of the chain of sentries, she dashed across fens and marshes for about fifteen miles and finally reached the house of a fellow Confederate sympathiser. Here she talked with a Southern officer and gave him her cypher. She then made her adventurous way back to her aunt's house, 'running the blockade' of the Federal sentries and 'dodging the odd bullet'.

Belle's exciting escapades were far from over. A few days later, while on her way back to Front Royal from Winchester, carrying letters for the Confederates, she was stopped by two northern detectives and searched. She had cleverly persuaded her travelling companion, a young Federal officer, unwittingly to carry the incriminating papers for her, but unfortunately they were discovered. Nevertheless the colonel's wrath was directed more at the innocent young lieutenant who had helped her than at Belle herself.

In May 1862 General Stonewall Jackson was preparing to recapture Front Royal when Belle was once again involved in her spying activities. She was sitting reading at the window of her room when one of the servants rushed in exclaiming that the Rebels were coming and the Yankees were preparing to leave town. She immediately went out into the street which was full of Federal troops milling about, approached an officer whom she recognised and asked what was happening. He explained that Jackson's forces had surprised and captured the outer pickets and were now within a mile of the town. He told her that they were about to set fire to the to the stores in the local ordnance depot and to move the artillery out of town. They would then withdraw, covering their retreat by burning bridges leading out of Front Royal and finally meet up with the main Federal army for a counter-attack against Jackson. Satisfied that she had some vital information, she felt it imperative to make contact with the Confederate troops. Putting on her sunbonnet, Belle ran down the street and into the open fields. She was fairly conspicuous in a blue dress topped by a small white apron – indeed a perfect target for the pickets:

> 'My escape was most providential, for, although I was not hit, the rifle balls flew thick and fast about me, and more than one hit the ground so near my feet as to throw dust in my eyes. Nor was this all; the Federals in the hospital, seeing in which direction the shots of their pickets were aimed, followed the example and opened fire on me. On this occasion my life was spared by what seemed to me then, and still seems, a little short of a miracle; for, besides the numerous bullets that whistled by my ears, several actually pierced different parts of my clothing; but not one touched my body....'

At one point she was blown to the ground by the force of the explosion of a shell that landed only twenty yards away, but got up unscathed and ran on. As she neared the Confederate lines she waved her bonnet at the troops who were amazed to see a woman on the battlefield. General Taylor described her arrival:

> 'On the march to Front Royal we had reached a wood extending from the mountain to the river, when a mounted officer from

the rear called Jackson's attention, who rode back with him. A moment later rushed out of the wood a young, rather well looking women, afterwards widely known as Belle Boyd. Breathless with speed and agitation, some time elapsed before she found her voice. Then with much volubility, she said that we were near Front Royal; that the town was full of Federals, whose camp was on the west side of the river, where they had guns in position to cover the bridges; that they believed Jackson to be west of Massenuttons, near Harrisonburg; that General Banks was at Winchester, where he was concentrating his widely scattered forces to meet Jackson's advance, which was expected some days later. All this she told with the precision of a staff officer making a report and it was true to the letter....'

Whether her information actually played a major part in the success of the battle is not certain, but the bridges were saved and Jackson was able to sweep on northwards to Harper's Ferry and almost to the Federal capital itself. Shortly after the battle Belle received the following note from General Jackson:

May 23rd 1862

Miss Belle Boyd
I thank you for myself and for the army, for the immense service that you have rendered your country today.

Hastily, I am your friend,
T. J. Jackson CSA

As one might expect, the incident caught the attention of the press on both sides, making her famous in the south and notorious in the north – one of the northern papers even described her as leading the Confederate attack 'sword in hand'. So when Front Royal was recaptured by the Union forces, Belle was placed under continuous surveillance. On 29 July 1862 she was arrested on the personal orders of Edwin N. Stanton, Secretary of War, and taken to the Old Capital prison in Washington.

Fortunately, Belle did not have to stay in prison for long – a month later she was released in a general exchange of prisoners and sent south-wards to Richmond where she was given a rousing reception. She even had a short interview with her hero, General Jackson, who said, 'God bless you my child.' After a second term in prison, where she nearly died from typhoid fever, she was banished from her home state for the rest of the war.

In March 1864, when still not quite twenty years old, she left the United States for England. Ostensibly she was recuperating from her illness, in actual fact she was carrying Confederate dispatches. But her luck was out this time and the ship in which she was travelling was captured by a Union cruiser. All the dispatches and letters had to be burnt just before capture – but she was still taken prisoner and this time banished to Canada on pain of death if she was ever recaptured. Belle shortly resumed her journey to London, but this time without any dispatches.

The episode of her capture on her original voyage had an intriguing twist. She fell in love with a Federal officer, who was in command of the steamer that conveyed her to prison. Lieutenant Sam Wylde Hardinge had been dismissed from the US Navy for 'neglect of duty', having allowed the captain of the rebel steamer, on which Belle had sailed, to escape. He followed Belle to London and they were married in St James Church, Piccadilly. Sadly the marriage did not last very long; Sam returned to America shortly after the wedding and was arrested and imprisoned for several months. Returning to London in February 1865, in poor health, he died before the end of the year, leaving Belle with a baby girl to support. It was then that she decided to write her memoirs in order to support herself. The book was published and gave her some financial relief, but not for long.

She had been helped in her literary endeavours by George Sala, a leading English journalist of the day, who had reported on the Civil War for the *Daily Telegraph*. He now helped her to begin a stage career and she made her début at the Theatre Royal, Manchester, as Pauline in *The Lady of Lyons*. Although not strictly beautiful, she was graceful and had a good figure and she did quite well, returning to the United States the following year on tour. Her New York début ensued but was confined to a single performance! From then on her acting career seems to have been limited to stock companies in Cincinnati, Houston and New Orleans.

Belle married again in New Orleans in 1869, ironically once again to a former Union officer of English birth named John Swainston Hammond. He was now a sales representative for a tea and coffee firm and for the next fifteen years Belle moved around with him as he visited most of the large cities in the country. They had four children, one of whom died in infancy. The marriage ended in divorce and in January 1885 Belle married a handsome twenty-four-year-old actor from Toledo, Ohio. They were soon in dire financial straits and so Belle went back to the stage, giving dramatic recitals of her wartime experiences.

She was a popular entertainer, but was impersonated so often that she had to carry credentials to prove she was the 'genuine Belle Boyd'! Four years later, at the age of fifty-six, she died of a heart attack in Wisconsin. She was buried with full military honours and lowered into her grave by four Union veterans.

Perhaps Belle's driving force was her fervent love of the Southern cause (which was so much at odds with her later actions in marrying two ex-Union soldiers), and it is best summed up by the final words in her autobiography: 'I firmly believe that in this fiery ordeal, in this suffering, misery and woe, the South is but undergoing a purification by fire and steel that will, in good time, and by His decree, work out its own aim.' Certainly no woman could have done more for the cause in which she so fervently believed than La Belle Rebelle.

CHAPTER 5

Following the Loved One

The majority of women who went into battle first put on uniform in order to follow their loved ones into the army or navy. In England, for example, their husbands or lovers might have been snatched away by the recruiting sergeant or press gang, usually when they were the worse for drink. Having accepted the 'King's Shilling', there was no way that these men could escape the army's clutches; so, for their women, the only drastic alternative to the possibility of never seeing the loved ones again was to follow them into the service. 'Pretty Polly Oliver' is a well-known example, her story being told in a popular song. She made the decision to 'list as a soldier and follow her love'. Yet although they may have been able to fool the recruiters by donning male clothing, there was no guarantee that they would be successful in finding their lost loves.

Others in this category were themselves press-ganged into uniform by their husbands or lovers, in some cases most unwillingly. The best that can be said is that they were probably safer under the protection of one man, rather than becoming the prey of many. Clearly it depended on the individual woman's personality and temperament as to how she adapted to the change of clothes and identity. This became even more important when the man was killed or deserted them. Some promptly transferred their affections to another 'protector', others continued to serve alone, still disguised as men, having presumably developed a liking for the strange life of the bivouac and battlefield.

These women chose the fighting life under the spur of the greatest of all human emotions – love. They included many brave, devoted and respectable married women who followed their husbands across the battle-fields of Europe and even further afield,* as army wives have done for

---

*We have already covered in more detail the subject of army wives and camp followers of all ages in our book *They Also Served*, G. & A. Forty, Midas Books, 1979.

centuries. We have chosen to relate just a few stories of these indomitable women, who showed great personal courage on the battlefield, refusing to be parted from their husbands despite many dangers.

Mother Ross, dragoon and sutleress

Christina Davies – also known as Mother Ross – is one of the most famous of the women who served as a private soldier, partly due to the fact that Daniel Defoe wrote her biography. She was born in Dublin in 1667, her father, Mr Cavanaugh, being a brewer who also owned a farm at Leslipp, which was run by her mother. Christina lived with her mother and although she was taught to read and write and become a good needlewoman, was very much an outdoor girl. She wrote: 'I used to get astride upon the horses and ride them barebacked about the fields and ditches, by which I once got a terrible fall and spoiled a grey mare given to my brother by our grandfather.'

When, in 1689, Irish Catholics took up arms to support the exiled James II in the Jacobite War, Mr Cavanaugh sold all his corn, equipped a troop of horse and joined the king. His daughter described an incident that occurred shortly after his departure:

'While my father bore arms for King James, the neighbouring Papists, in the time of divine service, came to and blocked up the church door of Leslipp, with butchers blocks and other lumber. My mother was then in church, I was at home. But hearing the noise, and fearing that my mother might receive some hurt, I snatched up a spit, and, thus armed, sallied forth to force my way and come to her assistance; but being resisted by a sergeant, I thrust my spit through the calf of his leg, removed the things which had blocked up the door, and called to my mother, bidding her to come away, for dinner was ready.'

She was arrested for wounding the sergeant but released shortly afterwards.

Because her father had joined King James, the authorities confiscated his lands and effects, so Christina went to live with an aunt in Dublin, who ran a public house. Four years later, when her aunt died, she inherited the inn. There she met Richard Welsh, a shy, good-looking young barman and general assistant, and after Christina had made the first overtures, they were married. For four years they were very happy. They had two sons and Christina was expecting her third child, when her hitherto faithful and devoted husband disappeared. Nearly a year passed without a word and Christina had almost given him up for dead, when she received a letter from him.

He explained that on the day of his disappearance he had met an old friend and been invited on board his ship for a drink. Having drunk far more than he was accustomed to, he had not noticed that the ship had sailed and they had reached Helveet Sluys before he could get ashore. Penniless and unable to get back to Ireland, he had enlisted in Lord Orrery's regiment of foot soldiers.

Christina was determined to get her husband back. Her second son had died, so, leaving her eldest with her mother and the youngest with a nurse, she handed over her public house into the care of friends. She then cut off her long hair, donned one of her husband's suits and went to the Golden Lost inn where recruitment was taking place. She enlisted, without any problems, in Captain Tichbourn's company of foot commanded by the Marquis de Pisare, under the name of Christopher Welsh, and was soon disembarking at Williamstadt in Holland. She took part in the battle of Landen and was wounded just above the ankle, writing afterwards: ' I heard the cannon play, and small shot rattled about me, which at first threw me into a sort of panic, having not been used such rough music.' Her wound kept her out of the fighting for two months.

During the summer of 1694 Christina was captured with others by the French and imprisoned at St Germain-en-Laye. Here she bumped into her cousin, Captain Cavanaugh, serving with the French army. To her immense relief he did not recognise her and about ten days later she was released with other prisoners and returned to her regiment.

The regiment spent the winter months in Gorkhum and Christina idled away the time flirting with the pretty daughter of a wealthy burgher. This harmless frolic led to a duel with a rival lover – a sergeant in her regiment – whom Christina wounded. The father of the lady in question procured Christina's release, paid her debts and even obtained her arrears of pay for her. Realising that she was treading on dangerous ground, Christina hastily left town, joined the 6th Dragoons commanded by Lord John Hay, and served throughout the campaign of 1695, including the siege of Namur.

After the Peace of Rijswick in 1697, the regiment disbanded and she returned to Ireland without hearing any mention of her husband. Back in Dublin none of her friends recognised her and, realising that she could not afford to pay off the nurse with whom she had left her youngest child, she decided to re-enlist. The War of the Spanish Succession broke out in 1701 and she rejoined her old regiment, the 6th Dragoons, who were again commanded by Lord John Hay, fighting with them at Nijmegen and at the siege of Venlo.

It was during the second attack at Schellenburg that she received a musket ball in the hip. It was deeply embedded and she only just managed to escape detection whilst she was in hospital. After the battle of Blenheim, in 1704, she was one of the guard taking some prisoners to Breda, when she at last met up with her long lost husband – in the embrace of a Dutch woman! Christina forgave him but refused to live with him for the time being, so they agreed to serve as fellow soldiers – she posing as his brother. In 1706, at Ramillies, although fighting through the hottest part of the battle, she escaped injury, but as the French retreated she was hit in the head by a fragment of mortar shell. She sustained a skull fracture and was taken to hospital where she remained for ten weeks. It was while she was in hospital that her sex was discovered.

Brigadier Preston, Lord Hay and her fellow soldiers were all astounded at the news. The brigadier presented her with a silk gown and the other officers made donations towards a wardrobe more fitting to her sex. Immediately after leaving hospital she and Richard were remarried, with great solemnity and in the presence of many fellow officers, 'who every one, at leaving, would kiss the bride and left me a piece of gold, some four or five, to put me in a way of life.'

At the siege of Ath she nursed the wounded and killed an enemy soldier just as he fired a musket at her, describing the incident thus:

'Both his shot and mine, with which I killed the soldier, were so exactly at a time that none could distinguish whether I fell by the recoil of the piece or the enemy's ball. My husband and some of his comrades ran to take me up and seeing the blood, imagined I was shot through the head, but I convinced them to the contrary by spitting out the ball and tooth into my hand.'

While they were in Ghent, Christina had a premature baby, which died. Not long afterwards she became a sutler, selling provisions to the soldiers, and was allowed to pitch her tent in front of the regiment instead of at the rear as was customary, frequently riding out on her mare on foraging expeditions.

Richard Welsh was killed at the battle of Mons in September 1709 and for the first time in battle Christina went to pieces. She was writhing and shrieking over Richard's body when a Captain Ross rode by and, moved by her grief, offered her his assistance, protesting that the poor woman's tears had touched him 'nearer than the loss of so many brave men'. Christina later said, 'This compassion from the Captain gave me the nickname Mother Ross, by which name I became better known than by that of my husband.'

Eleven weeks after Richard's death she remarried. His name was Hugh Jones, a Welsh grenadier who had long been making advances to her. The marriage proved very short, however, as he was killed at the siege of St Venant in 1710.

When the campaign ended, Christina went to London in the hopes of finding a benefactor. Queen Anne was petitioned and granted her a pension of a shilling a day for life, so she decided to return to Ireland. As she could not afford to travel by coach to Liverpool, she travelled northwards in a wagon with eight other women. They passed the time listening to Christina's wartime exploits but refused to believe a word of them! Not far from Coventry they were stopped by a highwayman who demanded their money. The other women, trembling with fear, hastened to comply to his demands, but Christina reprimanded him and said that they would only hand over what they could spare. The astonished highwayman, when he recovered his breath, replied that he would take all they had. As he leaned forward to collect their money in his hat, Christina furiously grabbed a pistol from his belt, cocked it and shot him, then hit him on the head with the butt, knocking him off his horse. She took his pistol, powder horn and, of course, his horse and saddle, then rode it triumphantly into Coventry, where she was publicly thanked by the mayor who collected £16 for her as a reward. She continued her journey and in Chester, where news of her exploit had preceded her, they handed her the sum of £11. Thanking the citizens, she remarked that she wished she could meet a highwayman every week!

Arriving in Dublin and unable to recover her public house, she set up a beer shop and was soon quite comfortably off; then she met and married her third husband – a soldier in the Welsh Fusiliers named Davies. After the wedding the regiment was posted to England, so Christina sold her business and went to London. Here she set up a similar shop in Willow Walk, Tothill Fields, Westminster, for the sale of 'strong liquor and farthing pies'. She was a very good businesswoman and was soon able to purchase her husband's release from the army. Imagine her annoyance when two days later, being stone drunk, he enlisted in the Guards. Towards the end of that year the Life and Foot Guards were camped in Hyde Park and Christina kept a sutler's tent there. She also marched in the funeral procession of the Duke of Marlborough 'with a heavy heart and streaming eyes'.

Her husband was again discharged but spent money so freely that she was obliged to sell her beer house in Paddington and then another one that she ran in Charles Street. She returned to Dublin for a while but was unable to settle and so bored that she came back to England in less than a year. She spent the next three years in Chester and then returned to London. Her husband finally became an inmate of the Royal Hospital, Chelsea, and so did Christina. Here she remained, supported by the kindness of the many officers who had known her as Mother Ross. She died in 1739 and was buried with full military honours in the churchyard of St Margaret's, Westminster.

Mary Schellenck

Mary Schellenck was born in Ghent, Belgium, in 1757. At the age of eight her father died and the girl then lived with her mother and a series of 'uncles' for the next few years. When her mother remarried, Mary was abandoned. She took a job as a serving maid in a tavern – a dreadful place from which she was soon dismissed, as her French was not good enough. In desperation she sold matches on the street until she was rescued by her stepbrother François Schellenck and her uncle Jean van Callenberg, a tailor, and went to live in his house. Here she fell in love with a weaver, François Desaegher, and pretended to be pregnant in order to get him to marry her, but he refused. At this moment her mother reappeared on the scene, having been deserted by her soldier husband. She took Mary back to Ghent and, realising that her daughter was similarly a girl of easy virtue, proceeded to exploit her. Mary was arrested and put in the house of correction of the Abbé de St Pierre. When released in 1779, she and François Desaegher were married, had a daughter and lived quite happily until 1790 when her husband enlisted in the Republican army. Mary followed him, dressed as a man. She was short, compact, with brown hair and eyes, an oval face and small mouth; and although she was unable to write she managed to join the 2nd Belgian Battalion.

The following year she was made a corporal and the year after, a sergeant. She fought bravely against the Austrians at the battle of Jemappes in 1792, where she suffered a gunshot wound to her left leg and no less than twelve sabre cuts on her nose, arms and head. She was taken prisoner but later released and returned to France where she was promoted to lieutenant by General Rosiers, as a reward for her outstanding bravery. When she had recovered from her wounds she returned to the front, and in 1796 fought with distinction at Arcola, being mentioned in army orders.

That same year she was authorised by General Soult to join a company of the Belgian 8th Light Regiment where she met and subsequently married Lieutenant Louis Joseph Decarnin. Having fought through both the Italian and German campaigns, Mary requested a pension in 1803 but this was not granted until 1807, when she left the service. Two years later Decarnin was also officially discharged because of his wounds and they lived together in Memin until Mary died in 1840, aged eighty-three. The death certificate described her as the widow of François-Emmanuel Desaegher, one of the witnesses to the document being Louis Joseph Decarnin – 'a retired Captain, aged sixty-four, no relation to the deceased'.

Mary was buried with full military honours which befitted her long service. These are the bare facts of her exploits but in her home town of Ghent, the addition of legend, handed down through the generations, has produced many variations. One such story says that, still troubled by her wounds at the age of fifty-two, she took the opportunity of presenting herself to the Emperor Napoleon when he came to Ghent, requesting a pension. When General Soult drew the emperor's attention to her, Napoleon removed his own Cross of the Knight of the Legion of Honour, and pinned it on Mary's chest, saying: 'Madame, I grant you a pension of 700 francs and make you a Knight of the Legion of Honour. Take from my hands the Cross of the brave, which you have so nobly conquered.' Then, turning to his officers, he continued: 'Gentlemen, show you respect to this courageous woman who is one of the glories of the Empire.'

After this event her exploits, including her enlistment, battle actions and decoration by Napoleon, were staged as a tableau at the local Belleville theatre.

Loreta Velázquez

Loreta Janeta Velázquez was born in Cuba in 1842 – daughter of a Spanish diplomat and his French-American wife. Her father, said to be descended from the great painter of the same name, was a very wealthy man and when Loreta was two, he left the diplomatic corps and took over a large plantation in Mexico which he had inherited. Unfortunately, the following year war broke out between the United States and Mexico, and Velázquez volunteered to fight for his adopted country. He took the precaution of packing off his family to the British island of St Lucia for their safety, but was unlucky enough to lose most of his plantation when Mexico was defeated in the war, as it lay in the area ceded to the victors. Not long after this misfortune, however, he inherited another, even larger estate and was soon richer than ever.

Loreta was educated at first by a tutor and then at an exclusive school in New Orleans, under the patronage and protection of the Sisters of Charity. She grew into a beautiful, headstrong girl, speaking both French and English fluently, in addition to her native Spanish, and having considerable acting ability, which was to prove useful in later life. In the normal way she was told by her parents that they had chosen a suitable young Spanish grandee for her to marry, but to their consternation she fell in love with a handsome young American officer, 'William X' (his name is not recorded in her autobiography).

They were secretly married in April 1856 when she was only fourteen years of age and her parents immediately disowned her. In the next four years Loreta had three children, all of whom died as babies, but despite these tragedies she was reasonably happy.

When the American Civil War began in 1861, William decided to fight for the southern states. The sentimental appeal of the Confederate cause clearly had a tremendous effect upon his wife, who begged to be allowed to fight alongside him, dressed as a man. William was absolutely against this strange proposal but soon had to join his regiment, leaving his wife free to pursue her madcap scheme. She purchased a Confederate uniform from a tailor in Memphis, disguised herself with a false moustache and beard, and, proceeding to Arkansas, set about raising a troop of soldiers, as that was the quickest way of obtaining a commission. She enrolled 236 men in four days and one can imagine her husband's surprise when Loreta triumphantly burst into his room at the barracks in Pensacola and told him of her success! In spite of his anger at this total disregard of his wishes, he must have realised that it would be impossible to change her mind. He agreed to keep her secret; so the Confederate cause now had a new recruit in the shape of 'Lieutenant Harry T. Burford' of the Independent Scouts. Poor William did not live to long enough to witness his wife's later triumphs, as he was accidentally killed when a carbine exploded on the ranges during musketry training.

As an independent officer of a troop of undisciplined volunteers, Harry Burford was not looked upon with much favour by the regular soldiers of the Confederate Army and she soon found barrack life irksome. She did not have to wait long, however, for the action she craved, when on 21 July 1861 she took part in the first battle of Bull Run. Throughout the day she was attached to the command of the fire-eating General Bee, whose rallying call to his men, 'See how Jackson stands like a stone wall', has gone down in history. Loreta wrote that the expression 'seemed to please the men mightily, for they took it up immediately, and with a cheer for "Stonewall" Jackson, they made another dash for the enemy.'

Although the Union forces were at first successful, the timely arrival of 4000 southern reinforcements, under General Kirby Smith, won the day for the Confederates. Indeed, had they pressed home their advantage they might even have captured the national capital, Washington. Loreta reckoned that the moment of victory was as good a time as any to ask for promotion, but she did not get it. In a huff, she set off for the Confederate capital, Richmond, to see if she could find some other way of gaining advancement. She hit upon the idea of becoming a spy in order 'to effect a coup that would make or mar my fortunes', but did not tell anyone in authority what she was planning, preferring to go it alone.

First she billeted her body-servant Bob at Leesburg, bidding him 'await his master's return', and then obtained suitable disguise. An old negress who did her washing was persuaded to provide her with a calico dress, shoes, sun-bonnet and woollen shawl. In this disguise Loreta bribed another negro to ferry her across the Potomac river to the Maryland side. It cost her twenty-five dollars and she had a miserably cold, wet crossing on a rainswept and windy October night. After spending the rest of the night in the shelter of a barn, she decided that she must try to get food and drink before proceeding further. At considerable risk she visited a nearby farm and told the owners of her journey from the south. Fortunately they were Confederate sympathisers and not only gave her food and advice on the best route to Washington, but also improved her costume by lending her articles from their own wardrobes. Thus fortified, Loreta set off again and soon reached her destination, slipping into the enemy capital without any problem, which says nothing at all for the northern counter-espionage organisation.

She took rooms at Brown's Hotel, bought new clothes and started to gather information. Apparently she had no difficulty in meeting with, and talking to, Union officers and clearly her good looks helped her. Although she did not learn any startling disclosures, she was able to use her considerable intelligence to make a reasonable story out of the gossip she collected. She came to the conclusion that the North were intending to mount an expedition to capture the upper Mississippi river area and to blockade the mouth of the river at New Orleans.

Considering that this information was sufficient to gain her the recognition she felt she deserved, Loreta again slipped through the defensive cordon round Washington – just as easily as she entered it – and headed back to Leesburg. Her mission had lasted several weeks; now she had to find someone to listen to her story. She again used her wiles to bluff her way into army headquarters and must have been not a little disappointed at the cool way in which her intelligence report was received. Her reward was to be assigned to the detective corps but she soon wearied of this and decided that she would join the army of Tennessee. Off she set, armed with some forged letters of introduction to the army commander, General Falk.

Loreta arrived in Fort Donelson just in time to see it surrender, playing her part in the battle, being on duty on the outworks when the Federals first attacked. She fought valiantly, helping to beat off wave after wave of the attackers, in sleet, snow and high winds of a bitter February in 1862; the battle went on without pause for forty-eight hours. Then 10,000 of the garrison made a desperate sortie and almost succeeded in breaking through, but Union reinforcements arrived and the Confederates were driven back in confusion. As the northern forces pressed home their advantage, it was decided that part of the garrison would stay and surrender, allowing the remainder to slip away to fight another day. The manoeuvre was successful and about 4000 escaped, leaving behind 13,000 of their comrades, together with a large number of field and heavy guns, so it was no small victory for the Union side. Luckily for her, Loreta Velázquez was not among their trophies.

Soon after this narrow escape, Loreta was wounded in the foot while out on patrol. The injury was not serious but sufficient to put her out of action for a time. She was inspected by a doctor and escaped detection, but decided that she would spend her convalescence in New Orleans. Unfortunately, this decision was to prove her undoing. From the start she was regarded with some suspicion in the town and was eventually arrested as a possible Union spy. She was able to refute the allegation easily enough but the following day was rearrested, taken to the provost-marshal's office and charged with being a woman in disguise. Loreta realised the game was up when she was conducted to the charity hospital for a medical examination, so she decided to come clean and told the doctor in charge the full story of her adventures. Perhaps she hoped to be applauded for her bravery; instead she was fined ten dollars and sentenced to gaol for ten days!

Undeterred by this shabby treatment, within days of her release from prison she had somehow managed to obtain more male clothing in order to re-enlist – this time as a private in the 21st Louisiana Regiment. But although she apparently got on well with her fellow infantry soldiers, Loreta did not intend to serve as a private and decided to try for a commission again. She managed this by producing her old commission, and was transferred to the army of East Tennessee.

In her new unit she was soon engaged in some dangerous fighting, leading patrols into enemy territory, and impressing her superiors by her cool bravery. One day, on yet another reconnaissance, her patrol was shelled and Loreta was badly wounded in the shoulder and right arm. She managed to get back to camp where, after some first aid, she was evacuated by ambulance and then hospital train. En route the train was delayed at Corinth and a surgeon arrived to look after the serious cases. Realising that she would not be able to fool him, she again told her story. He proved to be the perfect gentleman and arranged for her to receive private medical treatment, so that her secret was not disclosed to the military authorities.

At about this time Loreta met her second husband, Captain de Caulp, who hailed originally from Edinburgh. Loreta wrote:

> 'All these months that, in the guise of a man, I had been breaking young ladies' hearts by my fascinating figure and manner, my own woman's heart had an object upon which its affections were bestowed, and I was engaged to be married to a truly noble officer of the Confederate army, who knew me both as man and woman, but who little suspected that Lt Harry T. Burford and his intended wife, were one and the same person.'

Poor Loreta, her happiness was again short-lived, for de Caulp was killed in action shortly after their marriage.

Loreta did not fight in action again, but went on serving the Southern cause by travelling north and trying her hand at espionage once more. She endeavoured to organise a rebellion of Confederate prisoners of war in camps in Ohio and Indiana. She also stole electrotype impressions of Northern bond and note plates, so that the Confederates could make forgeries. During the last months of the war she travelled to Canada and Europe on semi-secret missions, arriving back in New York the day after Lee's surrender.

Although that was the end of her military career, she still had plenty more excitement ahead. She soon met her third husband – Major Wesson – who was organising an expedition into the jungles of Venezuela. Falling for his 'flaxen hair and blue eyes', she married him just before leaving the United States. Sadly, this marriage was also doomed to failure as the handsome major died of the 'black vomit' in Caracas, before the expedition proper could get under way.

Her fourth and final husband was a gold-miner, whom the restless Loreta met and married in Austin, Nevada whilst following the trail of the 'Forty Niners' westwards. The newly weds journeyed on to California, then to Utah, where she met Brigham Young and found him to be 'a pleasant, genial gentleman, with an excellent fund of humour and a captivating style of conversation'. A son was born in Utah before the little family moved on – and here in her own words is the end of her story: 'With my baby boy in my arms ... I started on a long journey through Colorado, New Mexico and Texas, hoping perhaps, but scarcely expecting to find, the opportunities which I had failed to find in Utah, Nevada and California....'

She concludes her autobiography by saying that she was not ashamed of her behaviour, hoping that her exploits would be judged with impartiality and candour and that she would be given credit for integrity of purpose: 'I did what I thought to be right, and while anxious for the good opinion of all honourable and right-thinking people, a consciousness of the purity of my motives will be an ample protection against the censure of those who may be disposed to be censorious.'

Susanna Dalbiac and Lady Juana Smith, heroines undisguised

Not all women resorted to male attire to be with their loved ones. Two wives of British serving officers performed acts of bravery in battle during the Peninsular War, but made no attempt to disguise their true identity.

Although army regulations in those days permitted only six wives of soldiers to travel with each company, the wives of officers were not so restricted – and many chose to accompany their husbands abroad. Mrs Susanna Dalbiac was the wife of James Charles Dalbiac, who was serving with the 4th Light Dragoons. Enlisting as a cornet (second lieutenant) in July 1793, he spent the whole of his military life with that regiment. He rose to the rank of lieutenant colonel in 1808, serving as second colonel to Lord Edward Somerset, who commanded the regiment when they landed in Portugal in April 1809. Three months later he led the left wing of his regiment in the famous charge at Talavera. He also took command of the regiment when Lord Somerset was absent, notably at the battles of Campo Mayor, Los Santos and Llerena. At the battle of Salamanca on 12 July 1812, the 4th Light Dragoons were a part of the force under General Le Marchant, and played their part in the famous charge in which the general was killed. It was during this battle that Susanna Dalbiac showed her remarkable coolness and bravery in action.

Susanna was the eldest daughter of Lieutenant Colonel John Dalton of Sleningford Hall, Ripon, in Yorkshire, and she married Charles Dalbiac in

1805. They had one daughter – Susanna Stephania – and when Charles was sent abroad with his regiment, Susanna and her daughter stayed at home; but how she longed to be with her husband. When Charles was taken ill with a fever in the summer of 1810, she hurried out to nurse him, and took such a liking to campaigning that she decided to stay with him. (One presumes her family looked after her daughter.)

Described by Napier as 'an English lady of gentle disposition and possessing a very delicate frame', she was always seen riding beside her husband 'upon an Andalusian steed'. Major W. J. Elliott wrote about her in an article entitled 'Heroism of Women in War' which was published in *The Illustrated Naval and Military Magazine* in the late 1890s:

> 'This gentle lady has followed her husband through two whole campaigns in the Spanish Peninsula. She has been by his side in every danger – in every vicissitude she has borne her loving share. In all the thrilling movements of the past few days she has ridden close to her husband's regiment. Again and again has he urged her to seek security but as often she has refused to leave him.'

The night before the battle, the regiment had bivouacked on the heights above the River Tormes, she sleeping 'wrapped in her husband's cavalry cloak'. During the night there was a violent thunderstorm and a number of the dragoons' horses broke away from their tethers and galloped wildly down the hill. At the time the Dalbiacs were sitting near some artillery guns a little farther down the slope and fortunately were not asleep. Charles was able to snatch up his wife, set her safely on top of one of the guns and then climb up himself, thus preventing them from being trampled by the frightened horses. A number of the dragoons were not so lucky – and thirty of the horses were still missing in the morning.

The turning point of the battle that took place the following day was the charge by Le Marchant's brigade. Susanna was in the thick of it, as Napier wrote: 'She rode deep amidst the enemy fire, trembling yet irresistibly impelled forwards by feelings more imperious than terror, more piercing than the fear of death.' This is how Major Elliott described her part in the action:

'Up the hillside then galloped the victorious Englishmen, the astounded enemy flying from their path in wild disorder, stooping under their horses' bodies to avoid the cuts and thrusts aimed at them, or running off to the hollows. Guns at the top of the slope now opened upon the somewhat broken horsemen. Madly the latter urged their chargers forward until they came to a stand-still from sheer fatigue. Yet with astonishing vigour, two squadrons, led by Lord Edward Somerset, galloped on until they reached the apex of the range and rushed upon the guns. Hurriedly the French gunners endeavoured to limber up and retreat. Too late! The English cavalry were among the cannons and five guns were captured in a moment.... The triumphant victors turned and took their trophies down the hill towards the cheering lines of infantry which were advancing to support this magnificent act of war.

'Is it creditable that amidst such scenes as these an English Lady, with features pale but set with a noble firmness, was watching anxiously the doings of her husband? Deep amidst the enemy's fire there rode this intrepid creature – Mrs Dalbiac – close to her husband's side at the head of his regiment.

'The cannon shot of the enemy flew past her, the French shells burst all around. Leaden bullets in their deadly flight pierced her riding habit in many places. Miraculously she had escaped so far without hurt. A shell burst close to her husband's side and he reeled for a moment in his saddle. Then a stifled shriek broke from her lips, but her husband recovered his seat and rode on in calmness. The cavalry trumpets rang out an order, the horses broke into a rapid trot, she drew aside her horse, for she knew that a desperate charge was at that moment to be delivered.

'As she watched the cavalry disappear in a cloud of dust and smoke, the infantry who were following up, came abreast of her. They were from Pakenham's 3rd Division. Susanna noticed that one of the sergeants of the colour guard had a nasty wound in his arm, and whilst he drank from her flask of wine,

she bandaged his arm.... She had saved the sergeant's life, for
he would have quickly bled to death but for this timely help.'

Again she pressed forward, handing her flask around to the many wounded
soldiers moving past her, until it was empty. She then refilled it from the
nearest stream and continued to give refreshment to the wounded, filling her
flask whenever she could, 'whilst a rain of bullets struck and splashed the
water in her face as she stooped to reach it'.

It was some hours after the battle was over before Susanna was able
to catch up with her husband, after an horrific journey across the battlefield
looking among the dead and dying, and praying all the time that he was safe:

> 'He gently lifted her from the saddle, and clasped her to his
> breast in thankfulness to God. Both had been wonderfully
> preserved from harm amidst all the terrible slaughter of the day
> of Salamanca. As the regiment was dismissed from its ranks,
> all its remaining men gathered around the brave lady with
> demonstrations of deepest admiration and respect. They came
> from the breasts of men whose feelings were hardened through
> constant danger, but they knew that a woman had shared with
> them the risk of violent death.'

Susanna continued to care for her husband and his soldiers until they
returned to England, and never again went on active service. Many years
later, writing to a friend, Charles wrote: 'Of this incomparable wife I will only
add that with a mind of the most refined cast, and with the frame of body
alas too delicate she was, when in the field, a stranger to personal fear.'

* * *

The second of our two heroic wives was in fact Spanish by birth, Juana
Maria de los Dolores de Leon – whom Kincaid described as follows on first
meeting her:

> 'Fourteen summers had not yet passed over her youthful coun-
> tenance, which was of a delicate freshness – more English than
> Spanish; her face though not perhaps rigidly beautiful, was

71

nevertheless so remarkably handsome and so irresistibly attractive, surmounting a figure cast in nature's fairest mould, that to look on her was to love her....'

Kincaid, however, was not the only man who fell in love with her at first meeting. In company with her elder sister, she had entered the British lines seeking protection, after the sacking of Badajos. Kincaid's companion was another officer in the 95th, Captain Harry Smith, and it was he who 'stepped in and won her'. The two girls had seen their home destroyed and had lost all their property – even their earrings had been wrenched from their ears, the blood still trickling down their necks – and did not know where they could go 'to lay down their heads, or where to go to get a change of raiment or a morsel of bread'. Gallantly the British officers promised to look after them and Harry Smith wooed and won the younger sister. Thirty-five years later he wrote: 'From that day to this she has been my guardian angel. She has shared with me the dangers and privations, the hardships and fatigues, of a restless life of war in every corner of the globe. No murmur has ever escaped her.'

Like Susanna Dalbiac, Juana accompanied her husband throughout the campaigns in the Peninsula and later with Wellington's victorious army, when they were advancing into south-western France during the early months of 1814. In his autobiography Harry Smith tells many stories about his wife, but one in particular shows most clearly what sort of woman she was. One dreadful night they sheltered from the cold and sleet in a little house where a poor French woman had given them shelter. Lighting a fire for them, she produced hot soup which she served from a very fine Sèvres slop-basin. She explained that the basin had been a wedding present which she had not used since her husband's death – she was, she added, a true royalist. They were suitably grateful for her kindness and the next day moved on. To their horror they discovered, after they had gone quite a distance, that the captain's servant had stolen the precious slop-basin. 'I said, How dare you sir, do anything of the sort?' He was normally an excellent servant. 'Lord sir he says why the French soldiers would have carried off the widow, an' she had been young and I thought it would be nice for the goat's milk in the morning.'

Angry at the theft, without her husband's knowledge, Juana saddled her horse and telling her groom, old West, that they were going to see an officer who had been wounded the day before, rode off. She was not back until late that evening, and Harry was very worried about her, when she at last arrived. She told him that she had ridden to the widow's cottage to return the slop-basin, and that the widow had '... cried exceedingly with joy, but insisted on her keeping the basin for milk, which my wife would on no account do. She had ridden that day thirty miles and had every reason to meet a French patrol.' When he asked her if she had not been afraid of being taken prisoner, Juana replied: 'No, I and West kept a good look-out, and no French dragoon could catch me on my Spanish horse, Tiny.'

After the Peninsular War Juana accompanied Harry and the regiment to Belgium where they were to join Wellington's army for the coming battle of Waterloo. Juana tells her own story : 'When the troops moved forward on the morning of the 18th June, I got on my horse and went towards Brussels, intending to wait the result of the pending battle....' She never actually got there. After a rather adventurous journey she finally arrived in Antwerp. On the following day, the 19th:

'In the afternoon we heard of the battle having been fought and won, but no news of my husband. So contrary to the wishes of my host and hostess, I ordered my horse to be ready at three o'clock in the morning, to rejoin my husband, what-ever shape fate had reduced him to.... Seeing some of our rifle soldiers, with an eagerness which may be imagined, I asked after my husband, when to my horror they told me that Brigade-Major Smith of the 95th was killed ... in a state of desperation I urged her [her horse Tiny] to the utmost speed for the field of battle to seek my husband's corpse.... In my agony of woe, I approached the awful field of Sunday's carnage, in mad search of Enrique, I saw signs of newly dug graves and then I imagined to myself Oh God he has been buried and I shall never again behold him. How can I describe my suspense, the horror of my sensations, my growing despair, the scene of carnage around me?'

Juana continued her grisly search until she met a friend, Charles Gore – ADC to Sir James Kempt, and asked him, 'Oh where is he? Where is my Enrique?'

Charles was able to tell her the glad news that Henry was alive and well in Bavay. Hardly believing in the miracle of finding that he was alive, Juana finally caught up with him: 'Soon, O gracious God, I sank into his embrace, exhausted, fatigued, happy and grateful – oh how grateful....'

Harry and Juana also served in campaigns in Canada, South Africa – where he because Chief of Staff under Sir Benjamin D'Urban – and India where Harry succeeded Sir Jasper Nicholls as Commander in Chief, also being made a KCB. The Smiths then returned to South Africa, where Harry was appointed Governor of the Cape Colony as Lt General Sir Harry Smith.

It is fitting that such a brave lady should have her name commemorated permanently by the famous town of Ladysmith in Natal Province which suffered so bravely under siege by the Boers (1899–1900).

Margaret Corbin, Fanny Doyle and Molly Pitcher – women at the guns

The United States Artillery is proud to number among its most famous gun crews three dauntless wives. The first, Margaret Corbin – who was known as 'Captain Moll' in the War of Independence – grew up on the Western frontier. She was orphaned at the age of five when her father was killed by Indians and her mother was taken captive. She was still quite young when she married John Corbin, of Proctor's Pennsylvanian Artillery, and, like other wives of that period, was allowed to accompany him throughout the campaigns of the Revolutionary War. She cooked, mended clothes and carried water to the wounded. She also took a great interest in her husband's artillery training and got him to teach her how to load and fire his cannon. She was with him during the defence of Fort Washington in November 1776 when the British fleet attacked the New York batteries. With upwards of 1200 cannon against them, the revolutionaries had little chance of victory. Under cover of a tremendous barrage, the redcoats stormed ashore and fought hand to hand with the gun-crews. When a matross was killed, Molly picked up his fallen rammer-staff and joined the gun crew. Her husband was killed shortly afterwards, but this did not stop her serving with the gun until the British troops scaled the ramparts and took the battered fortress.

Seriously wounded, with one arm nearly severed and a breast mangled by three grape-shot, Molly was taken prisoner. Remarkably, she recovered fully and was later released by the British on parole. She joined the Invalid Corps, a unit entirely composed of disabled veterans who did garrison, guard and even riot duties. In 1779 Congress voted her a small pension of half pay for life, together with an allowance for food and clothing. She is said to have protested violently when the normal liquor allowance was withheld and managed to persuade the general in charge to restore her rum issue! She is the only woman whose name is registered in the Corps of Invalids, and in 1926 her remains were reburied with full military honours in the National Cemetery at West Point. The headstone of Captain Molly's grave bears a bronze tablet depicting her firing a cannon.

Fanny Doyle's heroism took place at Fort Niagara, during the War of 1812. Her husband Andrew had been captured by the British at the battle of Queenstown Heights; as he was a Canadian by birth, he was taken to Montreal, tried for treason and sentenced to death. Fanny, who had rowed alone across the river and persuaded the British sentries that she should be allowed to attend her husband's trial, vowed vengeance.

On 21 November 1812, she arrived at the gates of Fort Niagara in the middle of an artillery duel with the British-held Fort George, and said to the commander: 'My name is Fanny Doyle, my husband was taken prisoner at Queenstown Heights. They have refused to parole him and sent him to Montreal. What can I do in his place?' Her request was not answered, so she took it upon herself to carry hot shot from the furnace to the guns, performing this duty all day without a break. In his official report on the battle the commander, Colonel McFeely, wrote: '... an instance of extraordinary bravery in a female ... I cannot pass over. During the most tremendous cannonading I have ever seen, she attended the 6 pounder on the mess house with red-hot shot, and showed fortitude equal to the Maid of Orleans.'

Our third and most famous artillerywoman, Mary Ludwig, was born in 1754 and was the daughter of a dairy farmer in New Jersey. Hers was a healthy outdoor life and by the time she was fifteen she was a strong, not uncomely girl, with a 'bold blue eye' and tousled red curls. She went into service as a domestic servant for the family of a Dr Irvine, who had a practice in Carlisle, Pennsylvania. He was an ardent nationalist and was later to become a general. He clearly imbued Mary with a strong sense of patriotism which was equalled only by that of a young neighbour – John Caspar Hays

– who worked as the local barber. The young couple met, fell in love and married in 1769.

Alas, their happiness was short-lived. Only six years later, soon after the War of Independence had begun, the young barber left his shop to become a commissioned gunner in Proctor's 1st Pennsylvanian Artillery. He had volunteered for a year and when his term of service ended, John decided to re-enlist, was enrolled in the 7th Pennsylvanian Regiment, and was sent to the company of a local officer, Captain John Alexander. Mary had continued her employment with the Irvines when her husband enlisted but her family invited her to come home. She felt that she had more chance of seeing her husband if she were in New Jersey, so despite the very real dangers that every traveller had to face in that area – deserters from the army, savage Indians and even enemy soldiers – she set off and arrived safely home.

Getting in touch with her husband's regiment, Mary decided to attach herself to it rather than stay with her parents. From then onwards she 'followed the flag', helping the wounded and in one instance actually carrying a wounded man to safety, after he had been left for dead. It was at this time that she became known as 'Molly Pitcher', presumably because she always carried a water jug or pitcher for the sick and wounded. One story about her concerns an incident when she needed help – to lift a very large and heavy camp kettle off the fire. She asked a passing soldier for help, which he gave so promptly that she asked his name. 'George Washington' came the reply – and that story is authenticated by the great man himself.

Molly Pitcher became a well-known figure on the battlefields, in a striped petticoat and an old gunner's coat, barefooted, with a battered cocked hat on top of her red curls. She not only looked after the wounded but also, on occasions, laid and fired cannons. During the battle at Fort Clinton, Molly was among the last to leave and helped to lay, train and fire at the oncoming line of British soldiers. The regiment, incidentally, was now commanded by her ex-employer Dr Irvine.

It was while taking part in the battle of Monmouth, in June 1778, that Molly was to win her place in history. The day had dawned scorchingly hot, with temperatures soon in the region of 100 degrees Fahrenheit. The veterans carefully husbanded the water in their canteens, refilling them whenever they could, from the streams they forded. Ammunition carts were weighed down with extra pails of water that would be needed to cool down the guns, which were already almost too hot to touch before they had even fired a single round. The battlefield was difficult for moving artillery, being cut by deep ravines and criss-crossed by thick woods.

The 7th Pennsylvanians were part of the column sent to help cover New York against a British attack. Commanded by General Charles Lee, the American troops were soon in trouble through mismanagement and lack of communications between Lee and Washington. At one stage they retreated from the field of battle which brought a severe rebuke from Washington in a flood of expletives which would have done credit to a sergeant-major. After the Commander in Chief had led his forces back to the field and eventual victory, Lee was court-martialled and suspended from command for a year.

John Hays found himself back as a member of a gun crew for the battle, as there had been considerable losses among the artillery in the days preceding Monmouth. It was hot, thirsty work and Molly did noble service, making countless trips to a small stream behind the fighting line in order to fetch water for the perspiring and thirsty soldiers. She was in a state of well-advanced pregnancy but that did not deter her. Then, to her horror, she saw that her husband's cannon had stopped firing and that her beloved lay amid the rest of the dead and wounded gun crew. The British redcoats were approaching and the Colonial line was in danger of breaking. Running forward to the gun, Molly, single handed, sponged out the barrel, reloaded and fired the piece.

It is said that her shot was a turning point in the battle. A scratch crew was hastily sent to assist Molly, who stayed on as a rammer, the line held and the British were beaten. Not until nightfall was she able to leave her post and attend to her badly wounded husband.

Hearing of the incident, General Washington sent for Molly and warmly commended her for her courage and devotion to duty. He gave her a gold piece as a souvenir and promoted her on the spot to sergeant. Her fame spread throughout the whole army and apparently the contingent of French troops serving with the Colonials spontaneously filled her hat with silver coins as she passed among them. Her American colleagues dubbed her 'Captain Molly'.

Some say that Molly's son was born in a tent on the battlefield, but in view of her strenuous activities that day it hardly seems likely that her pregnancy was that far advanced. In any event, it was her last battle, for her time was now fully occupied with her badly injured husband and, in due course, caring for her child as well. She continued to serve in the army for a further eight years as a cook and laundress at Carlisle Barracks. She was also employed as a children's nurse and seems at one stage to have had to depend on charity to make ends meet, which cannot have been very easy for a person of such determined and independent character. Her husband died in 1789 and she later married Sergeant George McCauley, who also died after a few years; Molly then went to keep house for Richard Miles in Carlisle. Her son carried on the family's military traditions and fought as a sergeant in the War of 1812.

Her considerable bravery and service to her country were eventually recognised when, in 1822, the Legislative Assembly of the State of Pennsylvania passed a bill, 'without one dissentient voice', granting her an immediate sum of forty dollars, 'with a similar sum half-yearly during her life'. The point was also made that this grant was for her services during the Revolutionary War and not because she was a soldier's widow. 'Captain Molly' lived another ten years, taking an interest in military activities, and passed away at the age of seventy-eight.

Her valour is now commemorated on a stone which was erected over her grave site at Carlisle, on the centenary of Independence Day, together with a flagstaff and cannon. A bronze bas-relief, depicting her as ramming the cannon, is also part of the Monument of the Battle of Monmouth. Molly Pitcher has been the subject of various paintings and she was further commemorated on a ten cent postcard which went on sale in September 1978.

Anita Garibaldi

Giuseppe Garibaldi, the Italian national hero, was almost as popular abroad as at home. At the height of his fame Abraham Lincoln offered him the rank of Major General in the American army; to celebrate the centenary of his victory in Sicily in 1860, his head was printed on stamps in both America and Russia. Even the reserved British people were roused to enthusiasm and he was warmly received on a visit to London. In Uruguay a statue of him as Commander in Chief of the Naval Forces of the Republic was erected in Montevideo harbour, and of course his name is perpetuated in the Garibaldi biscuit!

His twelve adventurous years in South America are little known to the average reader and yet he fought in two wars there: the first in the service of Rio Grande do Sul – a province of Brazil – and the second in Uruguay, against the attempted conquest by Argentina. It was also in South America, in Laguna, that he met and fell in love with the woman who was to be constantly at his side, regardless of discomfort or danger, throughout the twelve years of fighting – Anna Maria Ribeiro da Silva.

Giuseppe was born in Nice in 1807, the son of a merchant-captain. His parents had high hopes for him in a professional career, but at the age of fifteen he tried to run away to sea, so his reluctant parents allowed him to follow his chosen career. He started off as a cabin boy and by the age of twenty-four qualified as a merchant-captain in the Sardinian navy. He was devoted to Italy, joined the Young Italy movement, and after a vain attempt to raise a mutiny was compelled to escape to France. Forced to live in exile like so many other Italians, he sailed for South America where he captained a merchant vessel. From 1835–48 he spent most of his time at war.

Whilst fighting with the small Rio Grande navy, Garibaldi sailed into Laguna harbour – on 22 July 1839 – to bombard it from the sea, while the infantry forces under Canabara stormed it from the land side. By the end of the day Laguna was theirs. Living in the town at that time was young Anna Marie, commonly called Anita. She had been born in São Paulo, the daughter of Benito Ribeiro and Maria Antonia da Silva de Jesus - poor Brazilian peasants. Her father died while she was still a child and her mother moved the family to Laguna.

The local people, besides being fishermen, were extremely good horsemen and Anita learned to ride at an early age. She was described as being 'tall, a little stout with long protruding breasts, an oval face covered in freckles, and large black, slanting eyes and thick, flowing, black hair'. She was a strong, fearless girl and a good friend and neighbour described an incident which proved this point.

In 1835 a young male admirer waylaid Anita in a wood near Laguna, and tried to rape her. She fought back, snatched his whip, flogged him, jumped on his horse and rode to inform the police. It was because of this episode that Anita's mother pressurised her into marrying Manuel Duarte di Aquiar, a local shoemaker. They were married that same year in the church of Santa Antonio dos Anjos when she was about fourteen years old. Four years later she met Garibaldi.

In his memoirs Garibaldi wrote of their first meeting:

'We both remained enraptured and silent, gazing on each other like two people who had met before and seeking in each other's faces something which makes it easier to recall the forgotten past. At last I greeted her and said to her, "You must be mine." I could only speak a little Portuguese and uttered the bold words in Italian. But my insolence was magnetic. I had forced a tie, pronounced a decree, which only death could annul. I had come upon forbidden treasure, but yet a treasure of great price.'

At the end of 1839 Garibaldi was ordered to make a new raid on Brazilian shipping. His three ships – the *Rio Pardo*, *Seival* and *Cacapara* – slipped out of Laguna harbour under cover of darkness. Anita sailed with Garibaldi on the *Rio Pardo* towards São Paulo where they captured several merchant vessels. Returning from the raid, they met a Brazilian warship carrying seven guns to their one cannon and seeing that he could not escape the superior force, Garibaldi attacked.

After a fierce battle, in which Anita assisted with the guns despite entreaties to go below, the *Rio Pardo* and the *Seival* managed to get away, but they lost two of the merchant vessels they had previously captured. Knowing that the Brazilians would pursue him, Garibaldi landed just north of Laguna, transferred his cannon to the shore, hastily built some barricades and waited. The attack came at dawn and Garibaldi, now back on the *Rio Pardo*, and Grigg on the *Seival* defended from the harbour, assisted from the shore by a small group with the cannon. They suffered appalling casualties and many sailors lost their nerve but again Anita refused to budge, ignoring all requests to go below and spending the five hours of the battle firing a musket. She had a narrow escape when a cannon ball exploded near her, killing two sailors. Again Giuseppe pleaded with her to go below and she agreed to do so – in order to persuade the cowards who were hiding there to return to the battle, which they did. To their surprise, the enemy suddenly broke off the firing and sailed out of harbour. They later heard that the enemy commander had been killed.

The Brazilians, embarrassed by the loss of the battle of Laguna, now sent a new army, commanded by a brutal general, to retake the province of Santa Catarina. After fierce fighting, Garibaldi, Anita and the survivors joined up with the Rio Grande army, which was forced gradually to retreat during the following months. Anita continued to fight alongside Giuseppe, was taken prisoner, and escaped. She also found herself to be pregnant.

After several battles Garibaldi was sent to San Simon to supervise the building of ships, to be used in the next campaign. He and Anita rented a pleasant estancia and bought a herd of cattle. In September 1840 Anita gave birth to a son whom they named Manotti. By now Garibaldi was bored with his role in Rio Grande, asked for his release and was allowed to go. They took their herd of cattle and set off for Montevideo. Here, in 1842 (her first husband having died), they were married.

The next six years were comparatively normal for Anita in that she was keeping house and producing children – they now had three under five, Manotti, Rosita and Teresita. Unfortunately, while Giuseppe was away on an expedition, Rosita died, possibly a victim of an epidemic of scarlet fever in Montevideo during 1845 which caused a great many fatalities. When Anita produced a second son (Ricciotti) in 1847, they decided to return to Italy. Anita and the children, together with several other wives and children of Italian legionaries, left for Nice where Giuseppe's mother lived.

Garibaldi and his legionaries left several months later and when they put into a small Spanish port – Santa Pola, near Alicante – in the summer of 1848, they caught up with the news of rioting and revolt in Europe. Louis Philippe had been overthrown in Paris, Metternich, the Austrian chancellor, had resigned, and fighting had broken out in Italy.

Italy at this time was not a united country but a collection of independent and subject states. Austria had annexed Lombardy and Venetia; Sardinia-Piedmont was ruled, as it had been for 800 years, by the house of Savoy; Rome and central Italy were governed by the Papal states; the kingdom of Naples was a haven for criminals, usually in league with the corrupt police force; and the south was a poverty stricken and backward area, its administrators – churchmen – determined to keep the populace illiterate.

Garibaldi arrived in Nice to a great reception which both surprised and delighted him. He received the same tumultuous welcome from Anita, the children reunited after their six months' separation. During his few days in Nice he was guest of honour at a large banquet, declaring in his speech: 'You know I was never a supporter of the king. But I am a realist and I will join the king of Sardinia and if he will bring about a regeneration of our peninsula, I will shed my blood for him, and I am sure that all other Italians will think the same as I do....'

He was joined by over a hundred volunteers and sailed for Genoa. Anita begged to be allowed to go with him but he was adamant – the children needed her. He had agreed to help King Ferdinand recapture Sicily and when he arrived in Genoa he set about recruiting more volunteers. Soon he became preoccupied with more pressing events in Rome, which had declared itself a republic, and was beset on all sides by warring factions – Austrian, Neapolitan and Spanish troops – not to mention a recently landed army contingent from France, led by the new president, Louis Napoleon, nephew of Napoleon I, who was intent on becoming Napoleon III and restoring his uncle's empire. Garibaldi and his men were of invaluable help to the defenders. The legionaries now wore the distinctive red shirts that were to become the Garibaldi 'uniform'.

It was during a lull in the fighting as the French prepared their siege guns for battle that, to Garibaldi's great surprise, Anita arrived in Rome. Manotti, now eight, was at boarding school in Genoa; Teresita, three, and Ricciotti, eighteen months, had been left with friends in Nice. She had written to suggest she should join him but he had tried to prevent her. Now she demanded to be allowed to ride at his side as she had done in South America. When the siege guns came into action, it was only a matter of days before the city fell. Garibaldi, Anita and their gallant little army of defenders fought on to the end. When they could hold out no longer they left Rome with 4700 volunteers. Anita cut her hair short and donned men's clothing which consisted of a green uniform and a hat with a red feather in it.

Pursued by French, Austrian, Spanish, Tuscan and Neapolitan troops, the legionaries realised that they could not afford a confrontation, and having been refused asylum elsewhere they sought refuge in the tiny republic of San Marino. Leaving Anita and his now sadly reduced force of about 1800 men at the border, Garibaldi rode in and requested the San

Marino government to allow his men in as refugees, even volunteering to hand over their weapons. Agreement was reached but meanwhile the Austrians had caught up with the waiting legionaries. Demoralised by the lack of food and sleep and being constantly on the run, they fled. Anita desperately tried to stop them, calling them cowards, but to no avail. Garibaldi later wrote:

> 'The imposing presence of the American Amazon did not avail
> at San Marino, to stop the fugitives. The word "cowards",
> uttered by her in contempt, was borne away by the wind and no
> longer wounded the ears of men who had lost their spirit. Ah,
> I must recall the glorious fields of San Antonio to forget the
> disgrace of San Marino.'

The terms of surrender were: all weapons to be handed over to the Austrians, the horses to San Marino; Garibaldi and Anita allowed safe conduct to a port and thence to the United States; the rest of the legionaries to go home, or to leave the country if they were foreigners. Garibaldi rejected the terms and decided that they would escape. Unfortunately Anita, who until this time had been in perfect health and full of energy, suddenly became drained of strength and developed a fever. Needless to say, however, she refused to be left behind.

With the help of a guide they left San Marino in the dark of night with about 200 followers. Twenty miles south of Ravenna, in a small fishing village, Garibaldi decided to commandeer some fishing boats to take them to Venice. A violent gale delayed the launching of the boats by the reluctant fishermen for several hours, and they took to the sea just before the Austrians arrived. Anita was by now exhausted and feverish, and fifty miles south of Venice they ran into a patrol boat. Some of the boats managed to get to land, others were captured. About thirty of the legionaries landed on a marshy island; Anita, now too ill to walk, was assisted to the beach. They agreed to scatter and Garibaldi carried Anita to a cornfield where they rested in concealment. Her last coherent words to him were to look after the children. Realising that it was only a matter of time before they were caught, he made for a nearby farm, removed his red shirt and put on peasant clothing. He then carried the barely conscious Anita to the shore and bribed a boatman to take them to the mainland where they could find a doctor. Here they found shelter at a farm, but at the very moment Giuseppe laid his wife on a bed, prior to going for a doctor, she died.

Reluctantly leaving her to be buried by the farmer, Garibaldi made his escape. Grief-stricken by the death of his 'American Amazon', he later made arrangements for her body to be removed to Nice. In 1932 Anita's remains were taken to Rome, to be buried under her statue on the Janiculum.

Garibaldi survived to fight many more battles and made a great contribution as a propagandist for the unification of Italy.

CHAPTER 6

Women at Sea

From the seventeenth to the nineteenth century it was considered as almost a right of British seamen to entertain women on board ship, but officially it was only wives who were actually allowed to live aboard. Few captains, however, stuck rigidly to this rule, preferring to turn a blind eye rather than suffer mutiny or desertion. William III, for example, clearly condoned this action, as he wrote in his ship's order book '... requesting and directing the first lieutenant or commanding officer to see all strangers out of His Majesty's ship under my command, at gunfire, is by no means meant to restrain the officers and men from having either black or white women on board through the night, so long as the discipline is unhurt by the indulgence'.

In home ports the women lived permanently on board but in foreign stations they only spent the nights with the sailors, returning to their native villages during the day. One captain wrote in his diary in Antigua that he was absolutely horrified by the smells and squalor of the native villages, but '... bad smells don't hurt the sailor's appetite, each man possessing a temporary body, whose pride is her constancy to the man she chooses; and in this particular they are strictly so; I have known 350 women sup and sleep on board on a Sunday evening and return at daybreak to their different plantations.'

The sailors did not much care whether the women were black or white, and it was the practice of some captains, whilst in port in the West Indies, to enter into agreements with the local planters to supply a number of women every night. The native women were happy with the contract as it meant that they were well fed and looked after. In exchange they brought fresh coconuts and fruit on board with them. Some even hollowed out coconuts and filled them with rum – and it was a long time before this particular form of rum-running was discovered!

When the ship was ready to sail, the women were put ashore; most of them accepted this with resignation, only a few caused a fuss. Those who were left on board – subject to the discretion of the captain – were the official wives of well-behaved sailors and proved themselves invaluable during a battle, acting as powder monkeys and nurses for the wounded. Most of these women were remarkably brave and were often wounded themselves. Some even produced babies at this inconvenient time, these usually being named after the particular battle in progress during their birth.

There were other women who remained aboard without the captain's knowledge or consent – namely those who had put on sailors' uniforms and managed to fool their companions into thinking they were males. This is hard to believe in view of the extremely cramped conditions below decks on most warships in any age, and nowadays it would be completely impossible – due to the strict medical inspections – but apparently in those days it happened quite frequently.

Mary Anne Talbot

One woman who successfully disguised herself and became a seaman was Mary Anne Talbot. She was the natural daughter of Lord William Talbot, son of the Lord Chancellor and Colonel of the Glamorganshire Militia. Born in the parish of St Giles, London, in February 1778, she was the youngest of sixteen natural children whom her mother had by Lord William. Her mother died shortly after giving birth and Mary Anne was sent to a nurse who lived in the small village of Worthen, about twelve miles from Shrewsbury. At the age of five she was moved to Mrs Tapperley's boarding school in Chester, 'in order to receive a liberal education'.

She spent her spare time and holidays with her only surviving sisters, in whose company Mary Anne, as she put it later, 'enjoyed the only gleam of happiness' she ever experienced in her short life. It was her sister who told Mary Anne about her true parentage, explaining that before her liaison with Lord Talbot, her mother had been the Honourable Miss Dyer, a genteel woman of considerable dowry. Tragically, this beloved sister also died in childbirth and poor Mary Anne was passed on to the guardianship of a Mr Duker, whom she hated. He kept her in solitary confinement, seldom speaking to her and feeding her on scraps of food. He hoped by this strategy to get her to run away, leaving him in sole control of her considerable fortune – of which she knew nothing. But Mary Anne was too timid to take such an adventurous step, so he contrived to get rid of her to a Captain Essex Bowen, of the 82nd Regiment of Foot (much later this was to become the Queen's Lancashire Regiment), who was both suave and persuasive. His apparent kindness and flattering attention, coming after months of neglect and misery, overwhelmed the naive girl and she happily left with him for London.

She was introduced to all his friends as his charge and at first all seemed well; but, as Mary Anne later related, 'I soon experienced a visible change in the manners of my pretended protector ... who threw off the mask that had hitherto concealed his villainy, and placed in my view the determined ruffian.' Clearly the poor girl had suffered 'a fate worse than death' and when Captain Bowen received orders to embark for San Domingo, she was forced to accompany him, dressed as his foot-boy. They embarked at Falmouth on board the crown transport ship *Captain Bishop*, and sailed for the West Indies in March 1792, Mary Anne at this time being just fourteen years of age.

They had a hectic and unpleasant voyage with howling gales and tumultuous seas throughout the entire journey. To make matters worse, Mary Anne was fed on the scraps left by Bowen, so she was continually hungry; but she was also terrified by the thoughts of what would happen to her if the crew found out she was a female, so she resolved to 'suffer all with patience, rather than discover my sex'. Eventually they reached Port-au-Prince and after a few days she recovered her optimistic spirit and normal good health, avoiding as much as possible 'the sight and company of my destructive and abandoned betrayer'. They did not stay long in San Domingo as the regiment received fresh orders from the War Office to join the Duke of York's army in Europe. Mary Anne now underwent another change of character as Bowen realised that in order to keep her with him, she would have to be enrolled in his regiment. As he threatened to have her sold as a slave if she did not comply with his demands, Mary Anne was forced to enlist as John Taylor, a drummer. Drum Major Richardson gave her instructions in the 'art of beating the drum'.

They sailed to a port on the coast of Flanders, with Mary Anne having to carry out her duties as drummer as well as being Bowen's 'drudge and foot-boy'. She took part in the hotly contested battle of Valenciennes, and was wounded twice '... though fortunately neither deep nor dangerous; the first from a musket ball, which glancing between my breast and collar bone, struck my rib; and the other on the small of my back from the broad sword of an Austrian trooper'. Anxious to avoid detection and terrified of falling into an even worse situation, she elected to treat her own wounds by 'a process of self treatment, relying on the restorative properties of basilicon, lint and Dutch drops'.

Fortune at last smiled, briefly, on Mary Anne when Bowen, her persecutor, was killed. Despite everything she had suffered at his hands, she could not 'conceal the hidden character of a woman, in shedding tears on his fate, however unworthy'. While looking through Bowen's belongings she came across a bundle of letters revealing the conspiracy between Bowen and Duker to withhold her inheritance. Determined to have her revenge for all the years of impoverishment and discomfort, Mary Anne decided to desert the army.

Changing from drummer's kit back to her sailor's uniform, she set off for Calais, but she lost her bearings completely and found herself in Luxembourg. She arrived in September and there, 'through mere necessity, though sorely against my wishes', signed on with a Captain La Sage, commander of a French lugger, which set sail down the Rhine. To Mary Anne's chagrin, the vessel turned out to be a privateer with the aim of attacking English merchantmen!

After cruising for several months without much success, they encountered the English fleet, under the command of Lord Howe, in the Channel. According to Mary Anne:

> 'On our first sight of the British, La Sage ordered everyone to their duty; and observing me to be missing he followed me below to where I was concealed among the ballast ... and finding me persist in obstinate refusal to come on deck, he beat me about the back and sides with a rope, in a most inhuman manner ... but when on deck I absolutely refused to assist in the defence of his vessel.'

Fortunately for Mary Anne, the British captured the lugger and took her aboard Lord Howe's ship, *Queen Charlotte*, for questioning. She was able to convince her rescuers that she had not intended to fight against them, and was then assigned to the *Brunswick*, as a powder monkey, under Captain John Harvey '... where the story of my adventures, with the hardships I had suffered, gained me many friends'. Captain Harvey was most impressed by her cleanliness and as she was clearly different from the usual seamen, he questioned her closely about her previous life. Mary Anne did not tell him the complete story but he soon realised that she was a cut above the others in spite of her early misfortunes. He made her his principal cabin-boy and she served him in that capacity until they met the enemy in the battle of the Glorious 1st of June.

Mary Anne received several wounds during the battle:

'... a severe wound above the ankle of my left leg, by grape shot, that struck the aftermost brace of the gun, which rebounded on the deck, lodged in my leg; notwithstanding which I attempted to rise three times, but without effect ... to complete the misfortune, I received another wound by a musket ball, that went completely through my thigh, a little above the knee of the same leg, and lay in this crippled state till the engagement was over....'

The ship's surgeon found that 'after making me suffer the most excruciating pain', he could not extract the grapeshot from her ankle, so when the ship arrived at Spithead for repairs, she was taken to Haslar hospital at Gosport and placed under the care of a surgeon named Dodd. However, due to over-crowding, she was forced to be an outpatient, living at 2 Rienz Alley, Gosport, supporting herself on money she had received from the good Captain Harvey prior to the battle. Surgeon Dodd, despite his skill, was unable to extract the grapeshot without making Mary Anne a cripple for life, so it had to stay there.

After four months' convalescence she gradually regained a 'great measure of use of my leg' and she was discharged from hospital to serve on board Captain Thomlinson's *Vesuvius Bomb*. It was part of Sir Sidney Smith's command, which commenced a cruise in the hope of capturing French ships in the Mediterranean. But things did not go according to plan. The *Vesuvius Bomb*, separated from the other ships of the fleet in a gale off Dunkirk, was chased by two French privateers, who caught and boarded the English ship. In the mêlée that followed, Mary Anne was again captured together with a young midshipman named William Richards. They were taken on board one of the privateers and sailed into Dunkirk where they were put into St Clair prison. Mary Anne spent eighteen months in a prison cell, living on bread and water, hardly seeing daylight, and gained her freedom only when an exchange of prisoners was arranged.

Back in London, Mary Anne's adventures were far from over and she was soon on the American merchantman *Ariel*, bound for New York, employed '... in correcting the ship's books, paying the men, victualling the ship and taking in cargo'. They reached America in September 1796 and from New York she was invited by the captain to visit his home in Providence State, Rhode Island. Captain Field had a family of four children and a niece who lived with them. This niece took a fancy to Mary Anne and the forward young lady even went so far as to propose marriage. It was only with great difficulty that she managed to escape these designs!

Returning to England with the *Ariel*, Mary Anne and the mate John Jones went ashore in Wapping in plain seamen's dress and were attacked by a press-gang. Jones was able to prove that he was an American citizen but Mary Anne was only able to gain her release by revealing her sex, which was soon proved by a naval surgeon. Although everyone, of course, was dumbfounded at the news, Captain Field still tried to get her to go on the *Ariel*'s next voyage – but she declined.

She spent the rest of her life ashore, petitioning the navy for support, in view of her service and wounds. Although various subscriptions were raised on her behalf, and she appeared briefly on the stage in 'Babes in the Wood', she had to spend some time in the debtors' prison at Newgate, and eventually went into domestic service.

By a stroke of luck, she was taken on by the publisher Robert S. Kirby, who in 1800 published her adventures in the second volume of his *Wonderful Museum or Magazine of Remarkable Characters including all the Curiosities of Nature and Art*. After three years in domestic service she went into a general decline, partly due to her wounds and the hardships of her earlier days, and was soon unable to work. She was moved to the house of an acquaintance in Shropshire in December 1807 where she lingered for a few weeks. On 4 February 1808, at the age of only thirty, after an incredibly adventurous and tragic life, Mary Anne died.

She left as her epitaph the closing sentence of her short history in Kirby's *Wonderful Museum* – the pious hope that her story would 'serve as lesson to future guardians and those under their care, in avoiding the troubles I have experienced'.

Mary Read

On 20 November 1720, in the Court of Vice Admiralty at St Jago de la Vega, Jamaica, two women, Mary Read and Anne Bonny, were convicted of piracy. Their stories read like pure fiction but have been authenticated by many witnesses.

Mary Read was an Englishwoman whose mother had been married to a sea captain of some standing. Their first child was a boy and shortly after his birth the father went back to sea and never returned – whether he was shipwrecked, drowned or just absconded is not recorded, but the young widow was left to fend for herself. She was 'young and airy', failed to take sufficient care of herself, and soon found herself pregnant. Not wishing to explain her indiscretion to her missing husband's relatives, she made out that she was going to live with friends 'in the country' and left London with her one-year-old son. The little boy died soon afterwards and when the new baby arrived – a girl – she was named Mary.

Three years later, when Mary's mother had run out of money, she decided to return to her in-laws' home, passing off her small daughter as her dead son, hoping that her mother-in-law would provide their upkeep. Amazingly she was successful, so little Mary was brought up as a boy. One of her biographers relates that her mother let her into the secret 'when she had some sense' and she agreed to continue the deception in the hope of inheriting her grandmother's money, but when the trusting old lady died there was not a penny left. By then Mary was so used to wearing boy's clothing that she never entertained the idea of reverting to her proper sex. She was now thirteen years old and her mother hired her out as a foot-boy to a titled French lady. The job did not appeal to Mary; she was an active and restless girl and after a while ran off to the nearest port, where she 'entered as a powder-monkey on a ship of war'. So began her adventures.

The strict discipline and ordered routine of the man-o'-war did not suit Mary and although she stuck to it for a number of voyages, she finally deserted, went over to Flanders and joined the army. She joined a regiment of foot as a cadet, fighting bravely in various actions; but realising that she would never be able to afford to buy a commission, she transferred to a regiment of horse. If she was going to remain a private soldier she might as well ride rather than walk! She did well for a time but when she fell in love with a fellow trooper named Fleming, she began to neglect her duties. As they 'lay in the same tent' she eventually managed to let him discover that she was a woman, without appearing to have done so by design.

The revelation, needless to say, surprised and delighted him, thinking that she would immediately become his mistress. But Mary, not wishing to emulate her mother, insisted that he court her. When the campaign was over and the regiment returned to winter quarters, Mary bought some women's clothes and the two troopers were publicly married, doubtless causing a stir in the ranks! Mary's happiness lasted only a short time. The couple set themselves up at an inn called the Three Horseshoes, near the castle of Breda in Brabant, where they did good business, many of the officers taking their meals there. Then Mary's young husband died suddenly, and when in 1697 the Treaty of Rijswick was signed, the army departed, leaving the widow with no trade. Once again she put on men's clothing and made her way to Holland, enlisting in another regiment of foot. But there was little adventure or scope for advancement in peacetime so Mary did not stay long. Obtaining her discharge, she made her way to the nearest port and there joined the crew of a merchant ship bound for the West Indies.

The voyage ended in disaster, as the ship was captured by English pirates before it reached its destination. Finding that Mary was English, the buccaneers forcibly enrolled her as a pirate, and having plundered the merchant ship, they let it go. Shortly afterwards, a King's Proclamation was issued which pardoned all pirates who surrendered themselves to the authorities. The crew took advantage of this offer and for a time Mary lived quietly on shore. In 1718, however, with England and Spain again at war, she volunteered for service on a privateer, one of a number being fitted out by Captain Woodes Rogers, governor of the island of Providence, in order to cruise against Spanish vessels.

No sooner had the ship sailed than the crew mutinied and raised the 'Jolly Roger'. Mary Read was among the mutineers so once again she became a pirate, this time of her own choosing. The ship later came under the command of Captain Calico Jack Rackham who had a mistress named Anne Bonny, likewise masquerading as a pirate. When Anne made advances to the handsome new recruit, Mary was forced to disclose her true identity; and when Rackham became furiously jealous of Anne's supposed new lover and threatened to cut his throat, they quickly let him in on the secret. The flabbergasted captain, who now had two disguised women on board, kept the secret from the rest of the crew and the voyage continued. But soon came another twist to the tale.

When the pirates boarded a rival pirate ship called the *Star*, Mary fell in love at first sight with the first mate, Peter Hines, a young man on his first voyage who had been forcibly impressed into the buccaneers' crew, and covertly let him know that she was a woman. Marriage was out of the question, but having 'plighted their troth', they consummated their love in secret. When Peter quarrelled with another pirate, who challenged him to a duel, Mary realised immediately that he would be no match for the experienced cutthroat. She decided that she must intervene, but without branding her lover a coward. No stranger herself to duelling, having already fought two bouts, she deliberately picked a quarrel with the pirate in question and challenged him to fight her ashore, some two hours before he was to meet Hines. They fought with sword and pistol and Mary killed him on the spot.

Rackham's ship then continued its voyage, plundering both at sea and ashore. They captured two sloops, ravaged a schooner belonging to Captain Thomas Spenlow and landed on the island of Hispaniola, seizing a herd of cattle and two Frenchmen whom they later ransomed. But retribution was on its way. A government sloop commanded by Captain Jonathan Barnet – 'a known and experienced Stout, Brisk Man' – was hard on their heels and in October 1720 the two ships were joined in action. There could be no surrender as the alternative to fighting was a summary trial and a swift end on the gallows. The odds were too great for the pirates and their ship was captured. Mary Read and Anne Bonny, said to have been among the last to be taken, fighting with cutlasses on the blood-soaked deck, were finally chained and borne off to Jamaica for trial.

Mary made no bones about the fact that she had been a buccaneer, but stoutly protested that her lover, Hines, who had been forced to join the crew, should be considered a 'pressed man' and therefore innocent. The court agreed with her and he was set free. Mary was not so fortunate, and in view of her 'many and desperate' crimes she was found guilty and sentenced to be hanged. The sentence was held in abeyance as she was pregnant. But she was able to escape the noose. She contracted fever while in gaol and died before her child was born or the sentence could be put into effect.

Anne Bonny

Anne Bonny was Irish by birth, having been born in a small town near Cork. She also came from a respectable family, her father being an attorney at law – but Anne was illegitimate, her mother being a servant in the household who had 'obliged' her master while his wife was away in the country recovering from an illness. On her return she falsely accused Anne's mother of stealing silver spoons, as she had obviously guessed what had been going on in her absence. She was taken to prison to await trial at the assizes, and during this waiting period discovered that she was pregnant. Husband and wife had meanwhile had a furious quarrel over her treatment of the maid, and had parted company. But the wife apparently had a twinge of conscience and subsequently offered no evidence against her, so she was acquitted. Shortly afterwards she produced a daughter – Anne.

Her father now found out that his wife was also pregnant and, as he had not bedded her since the incident, realised that she had been unfaithful to him. Twins were born but the couple continued to live apart. Having developed a great affection for his bastard daughter Anne, the attorney took her into his home, but knowing that everyone in town knew of his affair with his servant, he dressed Anne as a boy and pretended that she was a relative's child, whom he was going to train as his clerk.

Meanwhile, to complicate the story further, the attorney's wealthy mother died, leaving all her money to his estranged wife and her illegitimate twins. She generously made him an allowance, but stopped it immediately she discovered that the child in his house was a girl not a boy, and, to make matters worse, the daughter of her former maid. Her enraged husband took Anne's mother back into his house and lived quite openly with her. Needless to say, this did not do his law practice much good and he decided to sell up and emigrate to America.

The couple settled in Carolina and after practising the law for a time he turned to commerce and made enough money to buy a large plantation.

When the woman who had passed as his wife died, Anne, now grown into a vigorous young woman, kept house for him. She had a fierce temper and various stories alluded to her violence.

All should have gone smoothly for Anne, because in spite of her confused background she stood to inherit her father's estate; but foolishly, without his consent, she married a penniless young seaman, and in his fury he drove her from home. The young couple took ship to the island of Providence where they hoped to find employment. Instead Anne met Captain Rackham, the pirate, who persuaded her to put on men's clothing and elope to sea with him. When she duly became pregnant, Rackham landed her on the island of Cuba, where she was looked after by friends until the baby was born. She then returned to Calico Jack.

It was at this time that the King's Proclamation was issued and Rackham and Anne, along with many others, surrendered and were pardoned. But they grew bored and soon took to buccaneering again, but with a difference. This time she was the real boss: 'And that same Anne, under the fitful gleam of the ship's lanterns, grim-lipped, eyes sparkling with determination, naked steel in fist, utterly ruthless and unscrupulous, the real soul of the enterprise, as brazen as it was desperate....' Together they embarked on a series of voyages that made them the scourge of the seas, feared by all who sailed those waters. Anne Bonny was always at Rackham's side, cutlass and pistol in hand, urging him on to even greater excesses.

As already told, their final voyage ended in capture. Rackham was condemned to death and granted a last request, which was to speak to Anne. She, it is said, gave him short shrift, remarking that if he had only fought better, then he need not now be 'hanged like a dog'. Anne, like Mary Read, was found to be pregnant at the time of her trial, so she too escaped the hangman's noose. No one knows what happened to her after the trial, but it is certain that she did not die in prison like her unfortunate sister-in-arms.

Hannah Snell, the brave marine

Hannah Snell came from a military background so perhaps it is not surprising to find her donning a uniform. Her grandfather, Samuel Snell, had fought in the Peninsular Wars, starting as a cadet. He was wounded severely in the Marlborough campaigns and was rewarded with a commission in the Welsh Fusiliers. He fought at Blenheim and Malplaquet, was wounded in both battles and finally died of his wounds.

His son showed no interest whatsoever in a military career, becoming a dyer and hosier with an establishment in Fryer Street, Worcester. He married and had a family of nine – three sons and six daughters – his second youngest daughter, Hannah, being born on St George's Day 1723. In no way a scholar, Hannah as a child was fascinated by stories of her grandfather's campaigns and always led the way in military games with her friends. Her parents died when she was a teenager and she went to live with an older sister, whose husband was a carpenter in Ship Street, Wapping.

During the Christmas celebrations of 1740, Hannah met James Summs, a young Dutch seaman, and fell in love for the first time. They were married in 1743 and seven months later James returned to sea. Hannah, by this time pregnant, at first ignored all suggestions that he had left her but later, having no news of him, began to suspect that it might be true. Her child was born but did not live very long, so Hannah decided to find her husband again. She stole a suit belonging to her brother-in-law and, using his name, went to enlist.

Charles Edward the Pretender had landed in Scotland and Hannah made her way north late in 1745 to the place where the army was concentrated. An enterprising recruiting corporal, having pressed a coin in her hand, declared that she was now legally enrolled. She then spent twenty-two days marching to Carlisle as one of Captain Miller's 'Company of Guise' Regiment of Foot. When they arrived in Carlisle and settled into camp life, Hannah fell foul of a sergeant who ordered her to assist him in the seduction of a young local girl. Instead, she duly warned the girl of his intentions. When he heard of this 'betrayal', the sergeant reported Hannah on a trumped-up charge of gross neglect of duty and she was sentenced to 400 lashes. Incredibly she withstood them without revealing her sex and with a stoicism that would have done credit to a strong man. The officer in charge was so impressed by her 'unflinching fortitude' that he spared her the final 100 lashes.

Shortly after this incident a new recruit arrived in the camp; his name was George Beck and he had been a neighbour in Wapping. Fearing that he would recognise her and realising that the sergeant would continue to find other forms of revenge, Hannah deserted. She stole some civilian clothes

Above: Brave Lady Arundel defending Wardour Castle. (Hulton Getty Picture Collection) *See page 25.*

elow: Joan of Arc. This evocative painting called 'The Maid', was painted by Frank Craig (1874–1918). (Hulton Getty Picture Collection) *See page 28.*

Left: 'Heroism of the Maid of Saragossa' from Cassell's *Illustrated History of England.* (Cassell) *See page 32.*

Above: The arrest of Louise Michel by Girardet. (Photographie Giraudon) *See page 37.*

Above: Belle Boyd, 'La Belle Rebelle'. (US National Archives) *See page 49.*

Right: Christina Davies ('Mother Ross') in the uniform of a trooper of the Scots Greys. (National Museums of Scotland) *See page 57.*

Above: Making a Charge! Loreta Janeta Velázquez, disguised as Lieutenant Harry T. Buford of the Confederate States Army, charging the enemy. The drawing is taken from a book entitled: *The Woman in Battle* by C. J. Worthington, late US Navy, which was published in 1876. (US Army Military History Institute Research Collection) *See page 63.*

Below: Molly Pitcher ramming her cannon, while her husband lies at the side of the gun, during the battle of Monmouth, 1778. She is said to have saved the gun from capture by the British. (US Army Field Artillery and Fort Sill Museum) *See page 74*

Above: Mary Anne Talbot in male attire, an 1804 portrait. (RHQ, The Queen's Lancashire Regiment) *See page 86.*

Right: A portrait [of]
Hannah Snell, 'drawn fro[m]
life at her own consent[']
(National Army Museum)
See page 9[.]

MARY ANNE TALBOT,

Who served Several Years

In His Majesty's Service by Sea & Land

In the Name of

JOHN TAYLOR,

Died Feb.ʳ 4ᵗʰ 1808, Aged 30

Publishd June 16. 1909 by R.S.Kirby London House Yard Paternoster Row

Above: Mary Anne Talbot.
(Adam Forty) *See page 86.*

Right: Mary Read kills
the sailor who challenged
her lover. (Adam Forty)
See page 91.

G.W. del.ᵗ   S. Sharpe s.

In the image: signature "*Léon Noël 1833*" (lower left), "*Lith. de Villain*" (lower right).

Below the portrait:

DOÑA CATALINA DE ERAUSO.

Monja alférez. The Nun Standard-bearer.

The original of this portrait painted in oils by the celebrated Pacheco in 1630 is to be found in Germany in the gallery of Colonel Berthold Stöppler.

Above: The Ensign Nun, Catalina de Erauso, from a portrait in oils by Pacheo, c. 1630. (British Museum) *See page 101.*

Right: A striking portrait of Thérèse Figueur in full uniform. (Photographie Bulloz) *See page 114.*

Sergeant Major Flora Sandes wearing her Kara George medal, Salonika, January 1917. (IWM – Q 32704) *See page 122.*

Left: James Barry in Jamaica, c. 1860. (RAMC Historical Museum) *See page 134.*

ight: Heroine of the viet Union, Senior eutenant of the Guards, tfina Gasheva was a avigator and flew over 50 sorties, dropping ore than 170 tons of mbs on the enemy in e Second World War. WM – RUS 5179)

The Chevalier d'Eon fighting a duel against the world champion, in front of HRH The Prince of Wales, 9 April 1787. (British

Young Russian girls, now soldiers in the 'Women's Battalion of Death', show off their cropped heads. (IWM – Q 106252) *See page 163.*

Left: Lucy Brewer, female marine – a somewhat fanciful drawing. (US National Archives) *See page 169.*

and set off by way of Liverpool, Chester and Winchester for Portsmouth. There she joined Frazer's Regiment of Marines and was posted to Captain Graham's company under the name of James Gray.

The Fleet, under the command of Admiral Boscawen, was being fitted out for service in the East Indies. Hannah was ordered to the sloop *Swallow*. The squadron had a dreadful voyage, with high winds and stormy seas through the Bay of Biscay, and encountered a hurricane off Gibraltar, where they had to put in for repairs before continuing their journey. Here Hannah was kept busy acting as a male nurse to her young master Lieutenant Wyegate, who had a serious attack of fever.

After the refit, the squadron set off again for India, calling at Madeira and the Cape of Good Hope. Off Mauritius – one of the French possessions they were hoping to attack – the Admiral debated as to whether to attack the main harbour, but realising that they had underestimated the strength of the fortifications and the alertness of the French troops, he held an officers' conference. They decided that as 'the reduction of the Island of Mauritius was not the principal design of the expedition, it would be better to abandon the attempt and push on to the Coromandel Coast'.

The Fleet sailed into Fort St David and were joined by other squadrons, bringing the total number of vessels to six sail of the line, four fifty-gun ships and others belonging to the East India Company, plus a military force of 5220 men, including 800 marines. Having docked, the marines disembarked at Areacopalong, a river fort, which they besieged for ten days before it surrendered. The British forces then went on to besiege Pondicherry. Hannah was one of the first to ford the river, breast-high and under continual fire from the French batteries. Her calmness and courage earned her praise from officers and men alike. During one of these skirmishes, having fired thirty-seven rounds, she received shots in both legs and a more severe one in the groin. She was taken to hospital in Cuddylorum, subsequent events being described in a chronicle written at a later date:

> 'After she was brought there and laid in a cot, she continued until the next day in the greatest agony and pain, the ball still remaining in the flesh of that wound in her groin; and how to extract it she knew not, for she had not discovered to the surgeons that she had any other wounds than those in her legs.

97

This wound being so painful, it almost drove her to the precipice of despair; she often thought of discovering herself, that by that means she might be freed from the unspeakable pain she endured by having the ball taken out by one of the surgeons; but the resolution was soon banished, and she resolved to run all risks, even at the hazard of her life, rather than that her sex should be known. Confirmed in this resolution she communicated her design to a black woman who waited on her, and who could get at the surgeon's medicines and desired her assistance, and her pain being so very great that she was unable to endure it much longer, she intended to try and experiment on herself, which was to endeavour to extract the ball out of that wound....'

The manner in which she intended to remove this ball was foolhardy and desperate. She probed the wound with her finger

'... till she came to where the ball lay, and then upon feeling it thrust in her finger and thumb and pulled it out. This was a very rough way of proceeding with one's own flesh, but of two evils as she thought, this was the least, so rather choosing to have her flesh tore and mangled rather than her sex discovered ... she made a perfect cure of the dangerous wound.'

After three months in hospital Hannah was discharged and enrolled as a deckhand on the *Eltham*, in which she sailed for Bombay. Falling foul of the dictatorial chief officer, who falsely accused her of stealing his shirt, she was clapped in irons for five days, and given twelve lashes, which punishment Hannah endured without a murmur. The *Eltham* was ordered home with but one main port of call – Lisbon – where they were to collect a large amount of money that was to be delivered to London. In Lisbon Hannah enquired as to the whereabouts of her husband, having heard rumours that he had been seen in the city. She discovered that she was too late; he had been publicly executed in Genoa some years previously, having committed a brutal murder.

When the *Eltham* was paid off in 1750, Hannah decided to return to Wapping. On taking her discharge she had a last drinking bout with her comrades and, having paid her reckoning like a man, announced: 'Gentlemen, you will never see your friend and fellow soldier, Jemmy Gray, any more.' Then she burst out laughing and continued: 'Why Gentlemen, Jemmy Gray will, before we part, cast his skin like a snake and become a new creature.' She then informed her silent and astounded friends: 'I am as much a woman as ever my mother was, and my name is Hannah Snell.'

The story soon swept the country. Having a good voice, she capitalised on her notoriety and briefly appeared on the stage of the Royalty Theatre in Wellclose Square. She appeared in an episode that was specially written for her; it recounted the story of her adventures as a soldier and sailor and she acted, clad once again as a male, as various characters. A newspaper of the time reported that 'in a most masterly and correct manner she went through the manual of platoon exercises, etc and sang several songs of a lively and diverting character'. A verse from one of them went:

> 'In the midst of blood and slaughter,
>   Bravely fighting for my King,
> Facing death from every quarter
>   Fame and conquest home to bring.
> Sure, you'll own 'tis more than common,
>   And the world proclaim it too,
> Never yet did any woman
>   More for love and glory do.'

Realising that her curiosity value was not going to last very long, she decided to take a public house. Various friends and some of her new admirers got up a petition on her behalf. The Duke of Cumberland is reputed to have been 'moved by her heroism, her unjust sufferings and her blameless life' and induced the king to grant her a pension of a shilling a day for life. Her sworn statement before the Lord Mayor of London, sent with the petition, read:

'An affidavit is published, which was taken before the Lord Mayor, 27th June, by Hannah Snell, born in Worcester in 1723, who took upon her the name of James Gray, bearing that – she served His Majesty as a soldier and sailor from November 27th

1745 to June 9th 1750; that she entered herself a marine in Captain Graham's company in Colonel Frazer's Regiment, and went to the East Indies on board the Swallow sloop of war, belonging to Admiral Boscawen's squadron; that she was present at the siege of Pondicherry, and all other sieges during the expedition; that she received twelve wounds, some of which were dangerous, and returned to England in the Eltham man of war, without the discovery of her sex.'

Hannah opened her public house in Wapping, which she called 'The Widow in Masquerade or the Female Warrior'. The signboard showed a picture of herself, one half dressed in marine's uniform, the other half in regimentals. Proposing to sell 'strong liquors at the best (lowest) prices', she appears to have been very successful, occasionally wearing male clothing, with sword and ruffles.

In November 1759, Hannah married a journeyman carpenter, named Samuel Eyles, in Newbury. After so much adventure, all she wanted now was a life of peace and quiet. They had a son who was fortunate enough to attract the attention and patronage of a rich lady of fashion, who had been fascinated by Hannah's exploits. She became the boy's godmother and gave him a good education and a start in life.

After Samuel Eyles died in 1772, Hannah married for the third time. Richard Hapgood was a prosperous man and all was set for Hannah to have a comfortable and happy old age. Unfortunately, after some sixteen contented years Hannah developed signs of insanity and by the end of the year had to be removed to Bethlehem Hospital for the insane. Here she lived quietly for three years, then died peacefully in her sleep on 8 February 1792 at the age of sixty-nine. She was buried in the grounds of Chelsea Hospital.

CHAPTER 7

Eternal Tomboys

Although Shakespeare used the term 'tomboy' to mean an immodest woman, we prefer the more usual definition of a high-spirited, romping girl who behaves like a boy. And what could be more appropriate for such a person, now out of girlhood but not willing to change or subdue her wilful nature, than to don male clothing, join an all-male society and take part in warfare, whatever the risks might be to life and limb. In this chapter we explore the lives of such bold, high-spirited women, who joined the military for the sheer hell of it and thoroughly enjoyed themselves in the process, although, to be fair to them, most had the good sense to own up to their charade when the going got really tough or they were in danger of being unmasked.

Catalina de Erauso, the ensign nun

Catalina de Erauso was known variously as Monja Alferes or the Ensign Nun. She was born in San Sebastian, Spain on 10 February 1592 and at the age of four her parents put her into a Dominican convent, the prioress of which was her aunt. There she remained until she was fifteen years old when, immediately before taking her vows as a nun, in March 1607, she ran away. Cutting her hair short and donning a suit of home-made man's clothing, she set off for the coast. Having fallen among thieves on the way, she joined this bloodthirsty group for several months and learned to use both a sword and pistol.

Before leaving Spain she decided to test her disguise by returning to San Sebastian and mingling with people she knew – she actually sat beside her mother in church and was unrecognised. Satisfied with her disguise, she travelled to San Lucar de Barrameda where she took ship for South America, serving as a cabin boy.

Because of bad weather, the ship was forced off course, ending up on the coast of Mexico. Abandoning ship in one of the Mexican ports, she became a bandit again and had many dangerous and bloody adventures. Eventually she left Mexico and headed for Lima, Peru, where she got a respectable job as a clerk. Unfortunately, having a violent temper, she was never able to remain in one place for very long. After several months in Lima she had a furious quarrel with someone, fought a duel – which she won – and was forced to escape the law. While on the run she killed one of her pursuers, maimed another, and evading the rest, reached Chile.

In 1619 she joined the army and was put into the company commanded by Captain Gonzales Rodrigues. Here she stayed for a few years, more or less out of trouble, expending her temper and energy in battle. Nevertheless, she did eventually have an argument – over a girl – with a fellow soldier and fought a duel. The friend missed, and Catalina, because she had fought a duel, was sent to prison in the fortress of Paicari. This massive fortress was situated in the middle of Indian territory and the inmates of the fort waged a continuous war against the Indians who pillaged, raped and ransacked the neighbouring countryside. Catalina joined in the fights with gay abandon and enthusiasm. On one occasion, when the Spanish were ambushed and lost their colours in the confusion, Catalina, with complete disregard for danger to life and limb, galloped her horse into the Indian camp and recovered the colours. She received a nasty wound in the shoulder, caused by a spear, but this heroic act was rewarded by a commission – as an ensign in Captain Alonso Moreno's company – and her release from prison.

Once again she appears to have had a peaceful few years with only minor disturbances, merely fighting when required so to do. Then inevitably her temper got the better of her and she fought another duel, this time running her adversary through with her sword. On the run yet again, she sought refuge with a woman whose husband, being of a jealous nature, chased, caught and wounded Catalina. She only escaped death by proving to the man that she, too, was a woman.

When she had recovered from her wound she made her way across the Andes to La Plata. Here she disfigured a woman in a brawl and was again imprisoned, but when her gaoler discovered that she, like him, hailed from San Sebastian, he allowed her to escape. Almost immediately she was captured by the dreaded government *corregidores*, but rather than be tortured, she admitted to being a woman and was put in a convent. Here she confessed to Bishop Carvajal, to expiate her conscience:

'I am a woman: I entered a convent when I was four, took the habit and was in the noviciate. When I was about to take my vows I ran away, changed my clothing, cut my hair and travelled around. I took ship, I gambled, I was unsettled, I killed, wounded and injured until now, when I fall at your Grace's feet.'

After several months in retreat with the nuns of Huamanga she transferred to a convent in Lima, travelling there on foot. She lived there, wearing a nun's habit, for two and a half years. Then, in 1624, being very bored, she went to Cartagena and asked to be returned to Spain. Highly delighted to be rid of their notorious member, the convent readily agreed and put her on board a ship bound for Spain. It had hardly left port when Catalina had a violent quarrel with one of the ship's officers, slashing him with a knife. She was finally overpowered and returned to shore. When she was next put aboard a ship she was kept locked up for the whole voyage.

King Philip granted her an audience, forgave her misdemeanours and gave her a pension of 70 pesos for life. Before settling down she decided to make a pilgrimage to Rome, to see the Pope. Having kissed the foot of Urban VIII she obtained pardon for all her sins, which she claimed were all due to her warlike character, and received permission to continue to wear man's clothing. After a few years of relative peace and quiet she again grew restive and at the age of forty-three resigned her ensignship and returned to South America. Here she disappeared into obscurity – but doubtless her last years were as troublesome as ever.

Sarah Taylor, the Manchester heroine

'On Friday last, a middle-aged woman applied for relief at the Churchwarden's offices in this town, and on being questioned as to her present situation, and her former life, she proved to be that description of Heroines, of which Hannah Snell and Christina Davies have cut so conspicuous a figure in English biography, and which Joan of Arc, and several others particularly in the revolutionary war, have done in that of France.'

So reads the opening paragraph of an article that appeared in the *Aston Exchange Herald* on 6 December 1814. The article continued:

'It appears that when a girl, she was in the habit of wearing boy's clothing, in which dress she served her father, William Roberts (who is a bricklayer) as a labourer; and being tall for her age, when about fourteen years old, she enlisted as a soldier into the 15th Light Dragoons. Probably her extreme youth and healthy appearance might occasion a laxity of attention, for she passed muster without her sex being discovered. In the course of two months, she learned her exercises sufficiently for all purposes of parade; the rough-riding master declared her the best rider with whom she was taught; which she imputes to the circumstance of having been used to mount, undaunted, to the top of high buildings, when attending her father.

'She remained with the 15th Light Dragoons in which she progressively attained the ranks of corporal and sergeant, for twenty-one years; her sex all the time remaining a secret to everyone. Perhaps the care she was under of guarding it, had the good effect of producing that regularity and orderly conduct which recommended the pretended 'William Roberts' to the favour and protection of the officers who procured her promotion. When she had been a soldier for twenty-one years, the colonel of the regiment tendered her discharge, which she demurred the acceptance of; but being under size, by her own consent, she was transferred to the 37th Regiment of Foot, which regiment she joined in 1800, at the island of St Vincent in the West Indies, where she was taken seriously ill (for the first time in her military career) of the yellow fever, when wanting some attentions which would inevitably lead to a discovery of her sex, she was obliged to entrust the secret she had so well kept to the wife of a sergeant, at a time when she was expecting nothing but death. She however recovered, and having no longer even nominal claim to manhood, she was obliged to resume feminine habiliments; but still enamoured of a military life, as she could no longer be a soldier herself, she became the wife of one, a private in the 37th of Foot, of the name of Taylor, by whom this Amazon had since had three children; still following the fortunes of war, through various climates; during which she was, with her husband, two years in a prison in France, from which they were released in July last, in consequence of the peace. On the day she landed from the cartel, her husband died and this Martial Heroine is now a widow, still anxious as she says, to follow a camp, as the most pleasant life of which she can now conceive.

'In the course of her military career she has visited many distant parts of the globe, and has been in many actions, and received several wounds, which however, were not severe, and were in parts of the body which did not betray her sex. A scar from a sabre, which graces her head, and a mark where a musket ball was extracted from her leg, are honourable testimonials of her service, but she says that the two years she spent in a French prison were far more difficult to support, and did her constitution more injuries than her voyages to the East and West Indies, her march from the Red Sea through Egypt or her campaigns in Flanders, in Spain and in Italy. She is however, in excellent spirits and "Fights her battles o'er again", with all the ardour of Goldsmith's old veteran who "Shouldered his crutch, and shew'd how fields were won".

'Having been informed by the Gentlemen in office, of the circumstances of such a woman, having been relieved at the overseer's board, the Writer of this article could not resist the curiosity, with which he was excited, which prompted him to see and converse with a Woman who had passed through life in so uncommon a manner. His curiosity was gratified; he found her an inmate in the house of her father, in Lee Street, Newton Lane; she and her aged mother were employed in washing linen in a room up one pair of stairs. He did not see the father, (who it appears had attended with the Heroine at the weekly board) but the mother fully corroborated all the circumstances of the daughter's story; which was repeated in the intervals of the washing operation. She is in full hope of obtaining the pension allowed to soldiers for long and faithful services; to which we think she is fully and fairly entitled. The proper testimonials, we understand, are sent up, to be laid before the Commander in Chief, in order to attain it as well as to procure the arrears of her husband's pay, which has accumulated whilst he was in the French prison.'

'We are aware that we have extended this article to an unusual length; but having been much entertained by a character so original, we thought we should gratify our Readers by a short sketch of the life of so extraordinary a Townswoman; for such a Woman seldom appears; to give life and interest to our local columns; and sure we are, that we shall be joined in the wish by all ranks of society, that the services of the soi-disant "William Roberts" may be remunerated in a pension to "Sarah Taylor".'

Both the Regimental History of the 15th Hussars and that of the 37th of Foot, which is now known as the Hampshire Regiment, contain similar stories to the one quoted above in such detail; so clearly Sarah was no figment of an inventive reporter's imagination. It is also interesting to note that her namesake, another Sarah Taylor, was the idol of the Tennessee Regiment during the American Civil War.

A Prussian heroine, Anne Sophia Detzliffin

Prussia has long been renowned for the fighting ability of its male soldiers, but women have not often figured in their armies, although in very early times there were Amazons among the tribes of the Allemanni, Marcomanni, Quadi and others who lived beyond the Rhine. The Roman historian Lucius Flaccus tells of the wives and daughters of these tribes who always accompanied their menfolk into battles. Although they did not fight, they stood on the sidelines, cheering on their men and urging them to fight more bravely. More than once they stopped a rout and obliged the warriors to turn and face the enemy rather than female ridicule. During the wars of Marcus Aurelius with the Marcomanni and Quadi, several women were found among the dead and dying, some of them even wearing armour.

A German woman warrior of a slightly more modern era was Anne Sophia Detzliffin who was born in 1738 at Treptow, about seventy-five miles north of Berlin. When she was nineteen she went to Colberg disguised as a man and enlisted in the local militia. They were a temporary force that had just been called into service at the beginning of the

Seven Years War, when the eastern part of Prussia was threatened with invasion by the Russians. After only six months' service with them she was clearly not getting the glory or excitement for which she thirsted, so she joined a regiment of cuirassiers who were part of Frederick the Great's regular army. Cuirassiers take their name from the heavy iron breastplate, or cuirass, which they wore as protection. They were the heavy cavalry of Frederick's army and direct descendants of the armoured knights of the Middle Ages. Each cuirassier carried a carbine, a brace of pistols and a broad, straight sword, double-edged and with a very large guard. In their straw-coloured coats, soft leather breeches, heavy riding boots, iron breastplate, embroidered accoutrements (such as the sabre-tache – a flat bag attached to the sabre belt), they must have looked a splendid sight, so perhaps Anne was drawn to them by this display of sartorial elegance! However, being a cavalryman in those days was no picnic either in or out of battle. She fought with them for two years in the many battles against the Austrians and Russians, and was in several fierce engagements, being wounded in the left arm by a sabre cut in one action near Bamberg, east of Frankfurt.

Anne next fought at the battle of Kunnersdorf, in 1759, which was won by the Prussians in spite of very heavy casualties. Her regiment returned to Saxony some days after the battle when she was taken danger-ously ill and had to be rushed to hospital in Neissen. When she recovered – without being found out – she was unable to rejoin the regiment as it had already left for a battle elsewhere. So she enlisted into the infantry and was posted to a grenadier company. Grenadiers were rather special in that they were usually chosen for some particularly difficult or dangerous task. Since they were employed in the thickest part of the fighting they invariably suffered the heaviest casualties.

It is interesting to note that the basic requirements for anyone wishing to join these élite troops were that they must be 'reliable, robust and mature'; and 'a grenadier should not have an effeminate aspect. On the contrary he must present a formidable sight, with a darkly tanned counte-nance, black hair and vigorous moustache; he must not appear too amiable or allow himself to laugh too easily.'

One wonders how Anne managed to fulfil all these conditions – especially the moustache! However, join them she did and fought as a grenadier in several bloody actions, including Strechlin and Torgau in 1760. In the latter engagement, fought on 3 November, she received two severe wounds in the head and was captured by the Austrians, who took her to hospital in Dresden. Again Anne managed to outwit the authorities and having made a partial recovery, escaped, slipped through the enemy lines and reached safety.

Once again she decided to change units, this time enlisting, in 1771, with a Colonel Colignon and his gang of 'free enterprise' recruiting agents with whom the Emperor Frederick had made a contract to supply recruits. Anne was sent to a regiment of Les Nobles Volontaires, who were probably the lowest of the low in army eyes. They were little better than brigands, given to drunkenness, thieving and displays of cowardice in battle. Little wonder that after only two months Anne found herself falsely accused of stealing fourteen pence from another mercenary and put under arrest. Anne was so incensed that she called for her own lieutenant and told him she was a woman, going on to declare that in all the years she had served with the cavalry, infantry and militia she had never once been under arrest or even received so much as a roasting for neglect of duty. This insult to her good name was more than she could stomach and she no longer wished to remain in the army – not that she would have been able to once she had disclosed her sex.

It is not clear why she chose to reveal her sex at that precise time but the punishments meted out were extremely harsh. One was 'running the gauntlet' where the offender was made to walk, stripped to the waist, between two ranks of soldiers who lashed him with water-soaked hazel wands. Another was the branding with the letter 'S' – standing for Spitzbube (rogue) – which then marked one for life. Perhaps, however, she was simply fed up with serving in such a bad unit after years with élite formations.

Nothing is known of her once she left the army but as she was still under twenty-four years of age, and after living such an eventful four years in the field, it seems difficult to imagine her settling down to domestic bliss!

Deborah Sampson Gannett, revolutionary soldier

Born on 17 December 1760, in the village of Plympton, near Plymouth, Massachusetts, of old pilgrim stock, Deborah was the eldest of six children. Her mother was deserted by her father, Jonathan Sampson, who ran off to sea, never to be seen again. Mrs Sampson found it difficult to raise her young family and the children had to be looked after by relatives and friends. Until she was ten Deborah had various homes and was then 'bound out' to become a servant to a farmer named Benjamin Thomas of Middlesborough, growing into a strong, capable young woman. She remained with this family until she was twenty (two years after she was legally free from her servitude) and being an adventurous lass who wished to travel without hindrance, made herself a suit of male attire, which she wore on frequent trips to the inns and hostelries of neighbouring towns.

The War of Independence had almost run its successful course. The winter of 1781–2 saw the American army very short of volunteers, and despite offers of cash bounties, they were not forthcoming. Deborah was clearly impressed by the appeal, and early in 1782, while staying with friends, slipped out of the house and enlisted – dressed in the clothes of a son of the household – under the name of Timothy Thayer, and was paid her bounty. Unfortunately, she spent a large amount of it in a tavern two miles from Middlesborough and then failed to appear at the regimental roll call the following morning. To make matters worse, she had been recognised, when she enlisted, by an old woman who was a neighbour of her former employer, Benjamin Thomas, and the authorities quickly sent officials to the Thomas's farm to confront her. She was forced to return what was left of the bounty, and told that if she tried to enlist again she would be severely punished.

This did not deter Deborah, who, walking first to Boston and then to Bellingham, bound her breasts flat, donned male clothes and again enlisted, on 20 May 1782, this time using the name of her brother – Robert Shurtleff. She was mustered in at Worcester three days later, to serve in Captain George Webb's company of the 4th Massachusetts Regiment. Moving on to the military fortress at West Point with the other new recruits, Deborah was issued with her basic uniform, musket and equipment and underwent basic military training. She must have had many problems in keeping her sex secret, as the washing and sanitary facilities were spartan in the extreme, but she managed to escape detection under cover of darkness. Her height, which was above average, strong features and stamina, clearly helped with her disguise.

Her first operational assignment was in June 1782, when she was a member of a detachment sent southwards to spy on the British, and later that month she was a member of an all-volunteer force sent to flush out armed Tories (settlers who still supported the British) in East Chester. Their camp was attacked early one morning and Deborah received her first wound. 'I considered this as a death wound, or as being the equivalent of it, as it must, I thought, lead to the discovery of my sex,' she wrote later. Covered in blood, mainly from a wound in the head, she was carried on horseback by a comrade some six miles to the French army hospital at Crompond. The French doctor treated her head wound and although he was clearly suspicious, he did not discover, nor did Deborah enlighten him, about the other wound in her thigh, where a musket ball had penetrated about two inches. Somehow she managed to procure a silver probe, lint and bandages, and after two unsuccessful attempts, extracted the ball herself – an act of sheer desperation. Later, having taken off her blood-stained uniform, she was wearing only a loose shirt, when the surgeon returned to see her. He was clearly worried about her condition, but she managed to convince him that she was just exhausted and all she needed was sleep. Before the wound in her thigh was completely healed, she was back with her regiment and marching to Fort Edward on the Hudson River, to stop Indian incursions against the settlements. She was in several battles against the Indians and saw some dreadful sights, with women and children among the mutilated corpses.

There were also many other skirmishes and even mutinies within the armies. In one an attack was made on the State House in Philadelphia, with artillery seized from the local barracks, which caused Congress to flee to Princetown. General Washington immediately sent 1500 troops under Major General Robert Howe to quash the revolt (mainly about pay and conditions). Deborah and four other soldiers were given leave to join Howe's force, but by the time they arrived the mutineers had dispersed. Shortly after her arrival, Deborah was stricken with 'a malignant fever which was raging in Philadelphia'. During his examination of her, Dr Barnabus Binney discovered her secret. Greatly perturbed, he had her removed to his house, but did not give away her secret even to members of his own family.

Fully recovered, her next military duty was as a member of a land survey expedition towards the Ohio River. On the way they stopped for provisions in Baltimore where a seventeen-year-old girl fell in love with the 'young soldier'. At first the embarrassed Deborah kept up the deception but later, wrestling with her conscience, she told the girl her guilty secret and, despite her shock and astonishment, they parted amicably and without anyone else being the wiser.

Peace came with the signing of the Treaty of Paris in September 1793, and Robert Shurtleff was ordered to West Point where the 4th Massachusetts were about to be disbanded. The Binneys saw her off from Philadelphia and she took with her a letter from the doctor to the West Point commander. En route the boat in which she was travelling capsized and although she could swim ashore, she lost most of her possessions. Dr Binney's letter explained her secret but when she presented it to General Paterson he refused to believe it – until Deborah put on her female clothing.

She was honourably discharged on 23 October 1783 and made her way to Boston. At Stoughton an uncle employed her on his farm, allowing her to assume the identity of her youngest brother Ephraim. In the spring of 1784, Deborah 'shifted to skirts' and married a local farmer, Benjamin Gannett. Between 1786 and 1790 she had three children – Earl, Mary and Patience – and she and her husband just managed to scrape a precarious existence. Lack of money led Deborah to petition the Massachusetts State Legislature for back pay which the army owed her. Her petition was upheld and she received £34.

A romanticised biography by Hermann Nann, to whom she had told her story, was published in 1797 under the title 'The Female Review'. This was followed by her appearance at the Federal Street Theatre in Boston in 1802. Here she talked about her army service, then, dressed in her uniform and carrying her musket, went through the manual of military drill (all twenty-seven manoeuvres) and finally sang a few songs. Despite these performances life did not become much easier for the struggling Gannetts, and in 1804 Paul Revere tried to help her with another petition to the Massachusetts representative in Congress. This, too, was successful; Deborah was placed on the Invalid Pension Roll and received four dollars a month pension. Although this did help they were soon back in debt and further petitions followed.

Deborah died on 29 April 1827, aged sixty-six, and was buried in Rockbridge cemetery, Sharon. After her death her husband also petitioned the Federal Government and Congress did eventually pass an 'Act for the relief of the heir of Deborah Gannett', approving on 7 July 1838 the sum of 80 dollars a year from 4 March 1831 until his death. Unfortunately, he died before this Act was approved.

The Fernig Sisters, a pair of heroines

The French Revolution aroused a wild and enthusiastic patriotic fervour in young and old alike and a desire to rid France once and for all enemies of the Republic. Women, in order to follow their husbands and lovers into battle, donned volunteers' uniforms and enrolled in their local battalions. Many of these brave, devoted women and girls died on the battlefields without their sex ever having been discovered; others were only found out when they were badly wounded and taken to hospital. Some went to war without putting on men's clothing and others, even though they did, were well known to be women by all who served with them. Among the last were the sisters Félicité and Théophile de Fernig. Although they dressed as men and acted as orderly officers on the staff of General Dumouriez, all their fellow comrades in arms knew that they were women.

Charles François du Périer Dumouriez, a general who enjoyed considerable popularity, had been appointed by the king to the office of Foreign Affairs, to satisfy the unrest and suspicions of the so-called patriots. He had courtly manners and a sharp wit, which hid his untrustworthiness. In her memoirs Madame Roland wrote:

'Dumouriez is active, vigilant, witty and brave, equally talented for war and for intrigue. Possessed of great military ability, he was the only man in France, even in the opinion of jealous colleagues, capable of commanding a large army properly. An adroit courtier, he was better fitted by his shifty disposition and dissoluteness to serve under the old court than under the new government.'

When the king declared war on Austria on 20 April 1792, it was Dumouriez, as a professional soldier, who was put in charge of the army.

The de Fernigs were a military family - the father was a captain of Dumouriez Guides and his son was a lieutenant in the regiment d'Auxerrois. They were natives of French Flanders and were driven from their home by the Austrians, who, among other atrocities, burned their home to the ground. After escaping from the Austrians, being homeless and uncertain of their future, the two de Fernig girls joined up with General Dumouriez's army, which was camped in the neighbourhood. The sisters were given uniforms, and presumably because of their father's influence, became aides-de-camp to the General.

During the battle of Valmy, in September 1792, they displayed such courage and gallantry against the Prussians that they were awarded horses and arms in honour of the Republic's splendid victory. It also gave Dumouriez tremendous prestige. He returned to Paris in a blaze of glory ostensibly to confer with the Executive Council, but actually, being an opportunist, to explore the political situation. On his return to the army he issued a proclamation urging all Belgians to unite and rise up against the Austrians. Many of them came to join his army, which then attacked the Austrians at Jemappes in November 1792. It was a hotly contested battle, the advantage swinging from one side to the other several times. Félicité acted as aide-de-camp to the Duc de Chartres – afterwards King Louis-Philippe – and Théophile acted in the same capacity to General Ferrand.

Whilst reviewing his troops before the battle commenced, General Dumouriez described the sisters as 'models of patriotism and auguries of victory'. Throughout the battle that followed their reckless bravery encouraged and inspired the soldiers, most of whom were raw recruits. The sight of these two fearless girls in the thick of battle acted as a stimulant on the young, impressionable soldiers, who felt that they had to emulate these two extraordinary sisters.

Before the overwhelming masses of General Clerfayt's cavalry, the regiments forming the centre of the French army gave way. The Duc de Chartres, his brother the Duc de Montpensier, accompanied by the sisters, then rode through the packed ranks of Austrian hussars, hacking their way through with their swords to rejoin their own infantry. The demoralised army was encouraged by the duke's rousing call, but more especially by the sight of Félicité de Fernig – a fragile girl of sixteen – bridle between her teeth, brandishing a pistol in each hand. They were exhorted to follow her lead and to emulate her. After many hours of fierce fighting, the Austrians were finally driven off. The capture of Mons followed, and after several more skirmishes the French entered Brussels. It was during one of these skirmishes, having extricated herself from a difficult situation, that Félicité rescued a young Belgian officer. He was being harassed from two directions by some Uhlans and fell from his horse when wounded. Félicité charged the Uhlans and shot two of them while the others scattered. With the help of some hussars from her regiment, she managed to convey the young man to hospital in Brussels.

After winning so many battles, General Dumouriez's star began to wane and he lost almost as many as he had previously won. He was accused of being a Girondist and of conspiring to rescue the former king, Louis XVI, who was about to go on trial. Realising that his position was shaky he tried to negotiate with the Austrians; but although he had been popular with his soldiers they were still patriotic and soon his army was in open mutiny. In hopes of settling the dispute, the General, the Duc de Chartres, Colonel Thouvenet, a small company of hussars and members of the general's staff – including Félicité and Théophile – set off for Condé. On their way they met some battalions of Versailles volunteers who, when commanded to halt, fired on the party. Dumouriez, amid flying bullets, escaped on foot across the canal and marshes. Théophile, her horse shot from under her, but unhurt, was joined by Félicité, who had given her horse to the Duc de Chartres. The two girls and most of their companions managed to cross the canal safely and here they all separated in different directions. As the girls knew this area quite well, they escaped on a ferry-boat to the Scheldt, taking with them Dumouriez and the duke. They returned to the French camp at Maulde but not long afterwards had to seek refuge with the Austrians (with General Clerfayt at his camp at Tournay).

The young Belgian officer whom Félicité had rescued and taken to hospital, recovered; unable to forget his charming rescuer, he set about finding her. She proved very difficult to trace as neither the officers nor men of her regiment had any idea of her whereabouts. He resigned his commission and, following leads, travelled through Belgium, France, Germany and Holland in search of her. When he was just about to give up in despair, he found her, with the rest of the family, in Denmark.

Félicité, now dressed becomingly in feminine clothing, was eagerly wooed and won by the young man and soon they were married and returned to Belgium. Théophile went with them to live in Brussels, where she studied music and wrote poetry for a few years, before dying at an early age. Félicité and her husband went on to live a quiet and happy life together.

Thérèse Figueur, the carefree dragoon

Thérèse Figueur, better known as 'Le Dragon sans Gêne' the carefree dragoon, was born in 1774 at Talmay, near Dijon, in eastern France. She served from 1793 to 1812 as dragoon in both the 15th and 9th Regiments; her documents show that she also served with the 8th Regiment of Hussars, between 1797 and 1798. When Napoleon's army was at its peak, there were thirty regiments of dragoons; and although the uniform had been somewhat simplified after the Revolution, it was, as Thérèse's picture shows, still splendidly elegant. Dragoons wore long green coats with different coloured lapel facings, cuff slashes and collars (Thérèse, for example, would have worn deep pink in the 15th and scarlet in the 9th regiment). Her magnificent helmet was of brass, with a tiger-skin turban and black flowing horsehair crest. Under the long coat was a white waistcoat and white breeches. Dragoons were the middle-piece cavalry, not wearing the heavy breastplate of the cuirassiers nor being as lightly equipped as the hussars and chasseurs. They were armed with a straight sabre, a pistol and a short musket (called a musketoon) of the 1777 pattern. Thérèse was a horsewoman of no mean standing and at one time or another had four horses killed under her.

One day the Committee of Public Safety issued an edict forbidding women, of whom there were quite a number, to remain serving in any of the regiments of the French army. Apparently all the generals and commissioned officers of the Army of the Pyrenees, in which Thérèse was then serving, petitioned the Committee that an exception be made of Citoyenne Thérèse Figueur and special authorisation was granted allowing her to remain in the service.

At the siege of Toulon in 1793 the citizens of the town had united with the English and Spanish fleets to oppose the Revolutionary government; Napoleon was commanding the French artillery in the attack on the fortifications. During this siege Thérèse was wounded in the left shoulder. It is said that she was put under arrest by Napoleon, during the siege, for being twenty-five minutes late for duty and that some years later when he became First Consul, he sent for the 'Dragon sans Gêne' to visit him at St Cloud. He paid her several compliments on her bravery and pledged her in 'a glass of something stronger than wine'.

She served in Italy, Germany and Spain where the French Dragoons won a tremendous reputation; she was also wounded at the battle of

Savigliano, receiving no less than four bullet wounds and sabre cuts. In July 1812, she was taken prisoner by guerrillas of the Curé Marino and sent off to England where she remained until peace was declared in 1814 – so she missed Napoleon's final battles before his imprisonment on Elba.

When she left the service, like her 'sisters in arms', Thérèse received only a modest pension, initially 100 francs, which was later changed to 200 francs. She was reputed to have been very generous and always helping others, remarkable for her 'piety, delicate tact, singleness of heart and self-forgetfulness.' At some date she had married a soldier called Clément Sutter, but by 1840 Thérèse was a widow and so was admitted into the Hospice des Menages (the local alms-houses) and spent her declining years visited by her faithful friends who 'delighted in hearing her military reminiscences'. In June 1861 the gallant dragoon died.

CHAPTER 8

In Father's Footsteps

The love of parents and family is often just as strong a bond as that forged between man and woman. Some women who joined the ranks were born and brought up in a military environment because their fathers were soldiers. Yet although they were fortunate to live in a family atmosphere, this was never easy because of the indifference shown by those in authority for even the basic necessities of life such as food and shelter. In the British army it was not until the 1790s that any proper barracks were built and that married soldiers were permitted to occupy small corners with their families. There they lived, cheek by jowl with the unmarried men, usually with just a thin screen of blankets or a piece of old canvas to separate their 'quarters' from the rest of the barrack room. Not the ideal way to bring up a family. Yet even then they were the lucky ones, because there was a strict limit to the number of families allowed to live in barracks – normally only six per company. The remainder had to fend for themselves, outside the gates, in the best way they could.

The rule was even more strictly applied when regiments were posted overseas, and harrowing scenes would be enacted as the wives drew lots to see who would be the lucky few to go with their menfolk and who would be cast adrift with no visible means of support, never knowing if they would ever see their loved ones again. Few could return to their family homes as the stigma attached to marrying a soldier made them social outcasts.

Under these circumstances it is hardly surprising that when a family did manage to be together they would fight tooth and nail to stay that way. If the husband was killed, it was incumbent upon the sorrowing wife to remarry, just as quickly as possible, in order to have another protector and provider for herself and her children. As a rule she had no lack of would-be suitors – even members of the burial party are known to have proposed on the way back from the cemetery, and to have had their offers gratefully accepted! If the wife died, then the father obviously had to employ every stratagem to keep his brood together as the alternatives were, at best, to see them fostered out if another family was available, and willing, to look after them; or at worst, for them to be set adrift to fend for themselves.

Young boys were often to be found serving in artillery bands or elsewhere in battalions as servants, so their chances of survival were that much better than girls. Consequently, a bereaved husband and father might well decide to disguise his daughter as a boy, so that he could keep her safely with him.

In the French army after the Revolution, whole families joined up together – fathers, mothers, sisters and brothers all going into the same regiment; so the presence of women in the army was not considered to be out of the ordinary. This practice continued until the Committee of Public Safety forbade women to remain in uniform, when the vast majority were forced to leave.

Phoebe Hessel, the little drummer

Phoebe Hessel was born in Stepney, London, in 1713; her father was a drummer in the British army and he managed to take his wife and young daughter with him when he went to serve in Flanders. The army at that time was deep in the doldrums after its spectacular successes against the French when, under Marlborough's great leadership, they had won splendid victories at Blenheim (1704), Ramillies (1706), Oudenarde (1708), and Malplaquet (1709). Even before the signing of the Peace of Utrecht in the year Phoebe was born, the British government was already cutting down the army and within a year Marlborough's army of 70,000 was down to around 8000. However, this was found to be totally insufficient to cope with commitments in the colonies and on the Continent, so the numbers rose to 22,000 - a reflection on Britain's emergence as a European power. Army discipline and conditions were still bad, especially abroad, and regiments often operated as individual private armies – the colonel being all-powerful. If he was rich and a humanitarian, his soldiers might be decently dressed and fed, otherwise they were ragged and half-starved. Composed, as it was, mainly of the dregs of society, a regiment was no place for a young girl without a strong protector.

Phoebe's mother died while her father was still serving in Flanders and the only way for him to keep his daughter with him was to disguise her as a boy. He taught her to play the drum and fife, finding her an adept pupil who 'quickly acquired great proficiency'. Bandboys were very common for many years, even up to the time of the South African War, so Phoebe's presence would have excited little comment while she was under her father's wing.

Whether or not she ever returned to England or whether he subsequently died is not recorded, but some years later she is said to have formed a strong attachment to one Samuel Golding, a private soldier in a regiment called 'Kirk's Lambs'. Golding was shortly ordered to the West Indies with his regiment and Phoebe was so smitten that she was determined to follow him at all costs. She enlisted into the 5th Regiment of Foot, then commanded by General Pearce, and embarked with them for Jamaica. This fact is recorded on her gravestone, as is the statement that she was later wounded at the battle of Fontenoy in 1745. The Fifth of Foot (the Royal Northumberland Fusiliers), however, did not fight at Fontenoy, so this part of the inscription is clearly wrong. As there is plenty of evidence to support the rest of her story it is probable that it was just an error on the part of the stonemason, who should have inscribed the Third of Foot (The Buffs).

Phoebe served for a number of years all over Europe and was badly wounded in the arm by a French bayonet at Fontenoy. When the doctor who treated her injuries after the battle discovered her sex, she was invalided out on a small pension and returned to England. She married Samuel Golding, who had also been discharged, and they lived together happily for over twenty years.

After his death she married a man named Hessel and bore him several children. She was living in Brighton when, in 1808, she met the Prince Regent during one of his frequent visits to his favourite watering place. At that time she was being maintained by some of Brighton's more benevolent citizens. Having heard her strange story, the prince asked what sum she required to make her comfortable. 'Half a guinea a week,' replied Phoebe, 'will make me as happy as a princess.' And so this annuity was paid to her for the rest of her life, by order of the Prince Regent – whom she called a 'jolly good fellow'. She was allowed to sell sweets, toys and pincushions, sitting at the corner of the Styne and Marine Parade, and became quite a tourist attraction. In her 102nd year, a large fête was organised to celebrate the victory of Waterloo, and being the town's oldest inhabitant, Phoebe was guest of honour, seated at the vicar's right hand.

Phoebe died in Brighton in 1821 at the ripe old age of 108, having lived through the reigns of no less than five monarchs. Her epitaph reads:

'Through fields of war for many a long campaign,
Where she fell sadly wounded by the slain,
Poor Phoebe strove to act the soldier's part,
A female form that held a manly heart.
At length, retiring from the battle's rage,
She lived to own a patriarchal age;
Staunch to her King, and to her country true,
May Heaven recruit her at the last review.'

Alexandrine Barreau, the Tarn grenadier

Alexandrine Rose Liberté Barreau, who was born at Sémalens in the department of Tarn, north-east of Toulouse, in May 1773, was enlisted at the age of nineteen together with her father and brother, into the 2nd Battalion, Tarn Grenadiers. It was one of the many new volunteer battalions raised to increase the size of the Army of the Republic in the early 1790s.

In line with other armies in Europe, France had adopted the system of forming élite battalions of grenadiers, and Alexandrine became one of these crack troops. It says much for her courage and tenacity because the grenadiers were always put where the fighting was hottest. One British officer wrote this about a French Grenadier battalion he fought against at Vittoria:

'They were the finest I ever saw, most beautifully clothed and equipped, the whole of them were dressed in sergeant's cloth with fine red shoulder knots. They wore tall bearskin caps and immense long feathers. They made a most formidable show in line. They were the first that were charged by our regiment and a proper example was made of them, they have hardly a man left to tell the story.'

She fought with the western army in the Pyrenees in 1793, where her report says that she conducted herself with great fearlessness, particularly in the battle of Briaton, while under the command of the 'immortal' Captain La Tour d'Auvergne. The gallant captain was then fifty and already had thirty-three years' service, having entered the Mousquetaires Noires, the élite of the Maison du Roi, as a private soldier. Alexandrine proved her bravery on numerous other occasions – notably at the storming of Alloqui, which was held in strength by the Spaniards. Her father and brother were both wounded alongside her and Alexandrine, having fired all her ammunition, drew her short curved sword and rallied the hesitant grenadiers. She was the third French soldier to enter the Spanish trenches and her example was such that the enemy was quickly put to flight. Once the fighting was over, Alexandrine returned to find her father and brother, and to nurse them back to health.

Inevitably she also married a soldier, named Layrac, and when he was wounded in action, she took over his cartouche (cartridge bag) and led his section into battle. She continued to serve until 10 September 1793 and thereafter had to petition to obtain a pension. Her petitions were accompanied by doctors' certificates verifying that she was now subject to violent headaches, poor sight and very weak hearing; moreover, that she had terrible rheumatics which meant she could not walk properly, all due to the bad weather and spartan living conditions which she had endured during her service in the army.

She was granted an annual pension of 100 francs from January 1819; thirteen years later, in company with her husband, she was allowed to enter the Avignon branch of the Hôtel des Invalides, a home for disabled old soldiers founded by Louis XIV. The headquarters was of course, in Paris, where 7000 aged and crippled former ex-soldiers lived. It now houses the tombs of such famous French soldiers as Napoleon, Foch and Leclerc. Alexandrine died peacefully in Avignon in January 1843, at the age of sixty-nine.

CHAPTER 9

The Professionals

Some women have approached the business of soldiering in a thoroughly professional way, proving their fighting ability on the battlefield and asserting their right to equality with their male counterparts without resort to disguise or deception. In a sense they were the true predecessors of our regular women's services of today, although they did not have to face the modern-day problem as to whether or not they should be armed. The two professionals included here carried weapons on the battlefield and knew how to use them, one receiving her adopted country's highest decoration for military bravery.

These women were respected by the men they served with in every sense of the term. The battlefield environment, where life could be ended at a moment's notice, inevitably aroused basic animal passions, and it might be expected that the 'brutal and licentious' soldiery, with their traditional reputation for rape and pillage, would have treated any females in their ranks with similar callousness, Strangely, this does not seem to have been the case with women soldiers, who were looked upon rather as comrades in arms than sex objects. It is debatable whether, in our more 'civilised' society, this would happen today were integration in the forces to be carried to its logical conclusion.

Flora Sandes: Nashi Engleskinja, 'Our Englishwoman'

'When a very small child I used to pray every night that I might wake up in the morning and find myself a boy.' These are the opening words of the autobiography of a remarkable woman who went to war for the first time when nearly forty years old, and who fought with the Serbian Army throughout the First World War. She was 'the lovely sergeant' – Flora Sandes – who wore male uniform yet did not try to conceal her sex. Her fellow soldiers looked on her as a great morale booster, and were pleased to have her in the fighting lines.

Flora was born in Suffolk in 1876, but spent most of her early days in Thornton Heath, London until the outbreak of the First World War. A week later, on 12 August 1914, she left England with six other nurses, all members of a privately raised ambulance unit under Madame Mabel Grouitch. Flora was not in fact a trained nurse, but had been an active member of the St John's Ambulance Brigade for three years, so had 'some of the rudiments of first aid'. It took them three weeks to reach Serbia and they found themselves working under the most difficult and primitive conditions, short of all the essential medical supplies. Their contract was only for three months (the authorities rather naively thinking that the war would quickly be over), after which time Flora returned to England, with the approval of the Serbian Red Cross, to try to raise money for medical supplies.

It was thanks to the 'power of the press' that her appeal letter, published in the *Daily Mail*, raised over £2000 in under three weeks. She spent it on the most vital necessities – gauze, cotton-wool, iodine, etc – 120 tons of supplies in all, which she and an American nurse, Miss Simmonds, who had returned to New York on a similar mission, then conveyed back to Serbia. It was now the beginning of February 1915, a typhus epidemic was raging through the country and thousands were dying. After working in Valjevo, a small town where practically the entire population was down with typhus, both nurses caught the fever but miraculously survived.

By mid-September the worst of the epidemic was over and Flora returned to England for a rest. She had only been home a few weeks when the news came through that the Bulgarians had declared war against Serbia, so she hurried back, heading for Monastir and her old Red Cross unit. On the way she volunteered for duty as a dresser to the ambulance of the Second Infantry Regiment, which was fighting at Baboona Pass near Monastir, trying to hold the road to Salonika open for the endless stream of refugees. The 'Iron Regiment', as it was called, comprised three battalions of about 1000 men each and was commanded by a Colonel Militch. It was regarded as the best unit in the Serbian army and Flora quickly grew very fond of the cheerful, simple soldiers. They saw nothing particularly strange about a woman being a soldier; indeed, Serbian peasant girls had from time to time served in the army, and in fact there was one currently attached to the regiment. What made them feel so much affection for Flora was that she was an Englishwoman, yet still prepared to fight for Serbia: 'To die for your country is not to die; but to die for someone else's country they thought to be something extra special....' So when the brigade which was holding the pass began to withdraw towards Albania, where there were no roads on which the ambulances could travel, Flora removed her Red Cross armband and said she would like to join the regiment as a private soldier. The commandant took the little brass figure 2s off his own epaulettes and fastened them on to her shoulder straps, calling her 'his new recruit'. Official sanction came later and as she wrote: 'For an English-woman to be fighting side by side with them seemed to please the soldiers immensely, and I soon became well known, the men always calling me 'Nashi Engleskinja' – 'Our Englishwoman'.

Flora Sandes's first taste of soldiering was a dangerous and difficult withdrawal across mountainous country in the depths of winter, constantly harried by a vicious enemy who tortured their prisoners and then slit their throats. She came under fire for the first time on Mount Chukas, during a diversionary operation in which her company endeavoured to draw the enemy away from the rest of the regiment. One of the soldiers lent her his rifle while he had a smoke – until then she had been armed only with a revolver; later she was to find that a carbine was the best weapon for her to carry, being lighter but just as accurate as a rifle. The company was short of food and water, so Flora came to the rescue, buying a quantity of corn meal which she had made into bread and gave every man in the company half a loaf and a couple of cigarettes as an 'English Christmas Box'.

Utterly exhausted, uniform in tatters but still with their morale high, the remnants of the company reached the Adriatic port of Durazzo. Much credit for their indomitable spirit was attributed to the presence of Flora Sandes, who was promoted to corporal and personally decorated by Crown Prince Alexander with the Sveti Sava medal during the New Year celebrations. Shortly afterwards, she was officially sworn in as a Serbian soldier, taking the oath of allegiance to Serbia and King. About a month later the complete Serbian army was withdrawn to Corfu and rekitted, mainly with British equipment, and Flora used her influence to get decent khaki uniforms for the men of the Iron Regiment. But Corfu was not a happy place for the Serbs for due to bumbling incompetence among the French officials there, no one could release the clothing and supplies the Serbs needed so desperately. Many of them died – over 150 each day at one stage. In the end, mainly thanks to Flora's endless hard work and patience, the authorities did release the supplies. Her comrades repaid her efforts by holding a special parade and presented her with the following address:

'To the High Esteemed Miss Flora Sandes

Esteemed Miss Sandes,

Soldiers of the Fourth Company, 1st Battalion, 2nd Infantry Regiment, 'Knjaza Nichaila', Moravian Division, 1st (Call) Reserves; touched with your nobleness, wish with this letter to pay their respects – and thankfulness to you; have chosen a committee to hand you this letter of thankfulness.

Miss Sandes. Serbian soldier is proud because in his midst he sees a noble daughter of England.... And you Miss Sandes should be proud that you are in a position to do a good, to help a Serbian soldier. Serbian soldier will always respect acts of your kindness and deep down in his heart will write your kind acts and remember them forever.'

It was signed by a number of representative sergeants, corporals and private soldiers, and the company commander added his own special postscripts. Soon after this very moving parade Flora was promoted again – to sergeant.

After a short spell of leave in England she returned to her regiment which was then on active service in the mountains of Macedonia. This was an even harder campaign than the previous one and the strength of the regiment was rapidly whittled down from 3000 to less than 500. Her greatest friend at that period was another sergeant named Miladin – a giant of a man who had sworn that she would never be taken prisoner if he could prevent it – unwilling to risk her being tortured. They shared everything but, like all the relationships that Flora had with her fellow soldiers, theirs was simply a bond of two comrades in arms. 'I cannot imagine,' she wrote 'anything more unlikely than to be insulted by a Serbian soldier.'

Flora was wounded by an enemy grenade during close-quarter fighting and temporarily blinded. One of her comrades saw her lying in no man's land and crawled back to her 'from under the very noses of the

Bulgars'. He was later aided by a sergeant-major and another soldier, both very small men, who could not carry her properly but gradually dragged her to safety. The next day they found ten of their wounded with their throats cut, lying in a row close to the spot where Flora had been hit.

The journey to the dressing station, in driving snow, took over two hours, so she was just about at the end of her tether when they arrived, with blood dripping through the bottom of the stretcher. Prior to setting out, she had half a bottle of brandy poured down her throat, a cigarette thrust into her mouth and her brand new corduroy breeches and shirt reduced to shreds by an over-enthusiastic medical orderly; she described herself as the 'raggedest, wettest and dirtiest looking soldier they had ever seen carried in'.

They gave her a hot drink, then laid her on the operating table to probe around for 'various pieces of bomb', without administering any form of anaesthetic. That proved to be a bit too much even for the tough Flora: 'I had to bury my nose in the broad chest of Doctor – who was standing at my head, while the other worked, and frankly yowled for the first time.' Instead of sympathy, however, he brusquely shoved a cigarette in her mouth and told her to remember she was a soldier. This, she remarked, had a far more sobering effect than any amount of petting would have had.

After the operation she went by stretcher to the Divisional Ambulance Station and thence, for two days, all the way down the mountain by stretcher and muleback to reach the nearest track where she could be transferred to a motor ambulance, and another day's indescribably rough driving to the rail-head at Vodena. From here she was taken by railway cattle truck on her last leg of the journey to Salonica. Arriving finally at the 41st General Hospital – a British Military Field Hospital for Serbian soldiers – she had the greatest difficulty persuading the British soldier on duty that she was a wounded Serbian sergeant and should be admitted, not a sick nursing sister to be sent on to the other side of town. 'Good God, another of them!' exclaimed the matron when she saw Flora; apparently a Serbian girl named Milunka, who was also a sergeant in the Iron Regiment, and had been injured earlier, was already in the same hospital.

The highspot of her stay in hospital was when the Prince Regent (later King Alexander) sent his ADC along to present her with the Kara George medal, the highest award a soldier in the Serbian army could receive, which carried with it automatic promotion to sergeant-major. She was discharged from hospital in the middle of January 1917 but it was clear that her wounds would not permit her to endure the rigours of army service for long and she had to go back to hospital for a further operation. This time the doctors would not allow her to resume active duties and she returned to England for two months' sick leave. There she launched another appeal – for clothes for the Serbian soldiers. She and the Hon. Mrs Haverfield, who had also been with the Serbs, together started the 'Sandes-Haverfield Canteen Fund' to provide 'tea gardens' (canteens) for the Serbian soldiers. She made speeches, appeared at concerts, auctioned her war souvenirs and gradually collected a considerable quantity of clothing and other materials.

A few days before her leave ended, Flora received orders to go to France for a three-week lecture tour to British soldiers on her exploits. She visited Calais, Le Havre, Le Touquet and many other places – each night in a different YMCA hut. Although she was enthusiastically received everywhere, Flora was determined that she was not going to spend the rest of the war talking about past battles, when there were still new ones to be fought; so back she went to Serbia with a friend, Miss Coates, who acted as chauffeur for their Ford car. She managed to rejoin her old unit and was with them when they had the satisfaction of seeing the enemy pushed out of their home area.

War ended shortly after Flora had rejoined her old company but her military career was far from over, and neither was her adventurous life. She took six weeks' leave in Yugoslavia:

> 'On this trip I looked for no adventure but I find that if there is one within a hundred miles – it comes straight for me! Anyway I got back from that six weeks trip feeling that whatever else life might be, it was never dull. I had chased Montenegrin brigands with a lorry; helped pacify a village in revolt; come down in a sea plane, which was left a total wreck on Lake Scutari whilst a French destroyer and a company of Serbs patrolled sea and land looking for us; had been shut up, in Fiume, for half a day by the Italians, because I was a Serbian sergeant, until rescued by a British captain.'

At the end of April 1919, the promotion lists came out and all the sergeant-majors who had been decorated were made up to second lieutenants, except for Flora. Although she was not particularly bothered about it, her comrades persuaded her to appeal; and astonishingly, a special Act of Parliament was passed to enable a commission to be given for the very first woman officer in the Serbian army. She continued to serve until 1922 when she was placed on the reserve list.

During the Second World War Flora lived in Belgrade, having married a Russian officer named Yuri Yuienitch, caring for him through a long protracted illness and giving English lessons to help with their finances. She told a reporter:

'I would sooner have spent this war at the front than in Belgrade. My worst experience was the American pattern bombing on Easter Sunday 1945, when I sheltered in a tiny shack and held the head of an old woman, telling her not to be frightened while the ceiling crashed down on my head. It was a dangerous moment too when Russian batteries just behind my house were firing at Germans across the Danube while the Germans on the other side replied. I must express my admiration for the Russians who took Belgrade without using artillery on the town and without wrecking a single house.'

By mid-1945 her husband was dead and she herself back in England, to spend her ten remaining years in her native Suffolk. She wrote:

'Sometimes now, when playing family bridge for threepence a hundred in an English drawing room, the memory of those wild, jolly nights comes over me and I am lost in another world. So far away it all seems now that I wonder whether it was really myself, or only something I dreamed.... I return to the prosaic drawing room and the realisation that I am a "lady" now and not a "soldier and a man".'

Yashka, peasant, exile and soldier

Marie Botchkareva, or Yashka as she was known to her army comrades, commander of the Russian Woman's 'Battalion of Death', was born in July 1889, the third daughter of a peasant family, in the province of Novgorod –

about 200 miles north of Moscow. The family were very poor and all lived in terror of their drunken, brutish father, always on the brink of starvation as he drank away what little money any of them was able to earn. Maria survived these terrible early years and grew up to have a strong constitution and a vivid personality. She tried to escape by marrying at fifteen – but the man proved to be a drunken lout like her father, so in trying to avoid one monster she found herself saddled with another. Finally she could stand him no longer and ran away to Irkutsk to live with a married sister. They, too, were very poor but Maria managed to get a job in charge of a gang of men and women laying asphalt at the Irkutsk prison. Although the appointment of a 'baba' (young woman) as a foreman produced laughter and ridicule, she soon proved her worth and was accepted. She earned good money and was reasonably happy, but after several months, worn out from too much hard work, she had a breakdown and was taken to hospital.

Unable to get her job back when she was better, she went to the employment agency and was sent to a woman 'looking for a servant' at 25 roubles a month for the right girl. But when she arrived at her new place of employment and was given a low-necked, transparent dress to wear, she realised to her horror that it was a brothel and that the 'kind lady' was the madame! 'Stars were shooting before my eyes – a house of shame! The thought pierced my mind and made me furious. I lost all my meekness and submissiveness. Seizing my clothes, I tore them madly to shreds, stamping my feet, cursing, shrieking and breaking everything I could get hold of....' Rushing off to the police station to make a complaint, she found that they were little better. She was saved by one of the brothel customers, a handsome young man named Yakov Buk, who had been impressed by her outburst the previous evening. He took her home to his parents who were very kind to her. Love blossomed between the two young people but was fraught with many problems. Caught by the authorities for hiding one of his friends – responsible for the death of a notorious governor of Siberia – Yakov was sent first to the central prison and then to four years in Siberia. That was in late 1912, but it was not until the following spring that the weather was suitable for moving the prisoners – murderers, forgers, thieves, students, officers, peasants and members of the professional classes who had transgressed against the tyrannical regime – to Siberia. Maria was allowed to go with Yakov in a party of about 1000, including twenty women.

They walked the first 135 miles, with very little food, then packed into a barge for the next 2000 miles – taking two months; here the men were put into Yakutsk prison and the wives who had volunteered to go with their husbands were released. When Yakov was sent to the prison 130 miles farther north in Anga, the stoical Maria went with him, the first Russian woman to go there. For a brief period they were almost happy but then Yasha began to accuse her of being unfaithful to him, tried once to hang her and beat her several times. This was more than she could bear so she ran away, cut off her hair, dressed in man's clothing and walked for six days all the way back to Yakutsk. After a few days' rest, off she set again and two months later she was back home. Her mother and family were delighted to see her, even her father, who had grown old and had mellowed.

It was now 1914 and Maria, determined to enlist, went to the HQ of the 25th Reserve Battalion, stationed at Tomsk: 'Enlist, eh?' laughed the Commander, 'but you are a baba, the regulations do not permit women to enlist. It is against the law.' Eventually, however, he was so impressed by her obvious sincerity that he suggested she send a telegram to the Tsar asking for his blessing. It cost her eight roubles but it was worth it. She was enlisted and kitted out:

> 'The Commander called in his orderly and instructed him to obtain a full soldier's outfit for me. I received two complete undergarments of coarse linen, two pairs of foot-rags, a laundry bag, a pair of boots, one pair of trousers, a belt, a regulation blouse, a pair of epaulettes, a cap with the insignia on it, two cartridge pockets and a rifle. My hair was clipped short.'

When Maria appeared in the barracks for the first time in full military attire, she was greeted with incredulous laughter from the rest of the raw recruits. That was nothing compared with the indignities she had suffered during her first night in a barrack room. The other soldiers presumed that she was a 'woman of loose morals' and she spent a sleepless night defending herself against the advances of would-be seducers. She soon ceased to be a novelty, however, and was accepted. She took the name Yashka, proved to be an apt student and came to like the ignorant, good-natured soldiers – once they had stopped baiting her.

Early in 1915 the regiment received orders to prepare to go to the front. The men were given a week's leave before departing and most spent it in 'drink and revelry'. Afterwards they boarded a troop train and moved up to join the Second Army in the Polotsk area:

> 'We were assigned to the Fifth Corps. Before we started the news spread that there was a woman in our regiment. Curiosity was at once aroused. Knots of soldiers gathered around my "teplushka" (the railway van in which they had travelled) peeping through the door and cracks in the sides to verify, with their own eyes, the incredible news.'

Yashka was soon in action, proving herself a brave and resourceful soldier, and after rescuing no less than fifty wounded from 'No Man's Land', she was recommended for an Order of the 4th Degree 'for distinguished valour shown in the saving of many lives under fire'. She was wounded herself, in the right leg, during a night attack and spent four hours isolated between friendly and enemy lines before being rescued and taken to a first aid post and then hospital. From there she went by hospital train to Kiev, arriving around Easter 1915; after two months' care and attention she was pronounced fit to return to the front.

Towards the end of the year Yashka had another session in hospital, suffering from a frostbitten right foot; the following year she was shot through the right leg and severely wounded. This time she was taken to hospital in Moscow and was out of action until the following June:

> 'Finally, one day at the beginning of June I was declared fit to return to the fighting line. My regiment had just been transferred to the Lutsk front. On June 20th I caught up with it ... it was midsummer and the heat was prostrating ... many of our number collapsed ... but the Commander implored us to keep up.... We occupied abandoned German trenches and at four in the morning we received word that the Germans had left their positions and started for our side ... we met them with repeated volleys and when they approached our positions we climbed out and charged them with fixed bayonets.'

During this charge Yashka was again seriously wounded, this time by a shell fragment in her spinal column, which paralysed her. The doctor at the dressing station was convinced that she would never survive, but again she proved them wrong and, after four months in the Moscow hospital, slowly regained the use of her limbs. At the end of six months she was fit again and despite having a piece of shell lodged in her omentum, she went back to war. She was rewarded with another medal – a Cross of the 3rd Degree – and was also promoted to senior non-commissioned officer, in charge of a platoon of seventy men.

It was now February 1917 and the soldiers at the front were completely unprepared for the events that were occurring far from the front – namely the Russian Revolution and the overthrow of the Tsar's rule. There was a good deal of unrest and indiscipline but gradually order was restored, Tsarist officers being replaced by those of the revolution. It was at this time that Yashka got the idea of forming a fighting unit composed entirely of women, to be called the 'Battalion of Death'. After considerable opposition she managed to get her proposal approved. There was no shortage of volunteers. Yashka appeared at the Maryinsky Theatre in May 1917 and appealed for 'women whose hearts are loyal, souls are pure, whose aims are high'. She recruited 1500 volunteers that first evening.

By 26 May 2000 suitable recruits had been chosen from the flood of volunteers and Yashka set about making them into soldiers. They were divided into two battalions of 1000 each, then sub-divided into companies and platoons. A male soldier instructor was allocated to each platoon and an officer in command of each company. One spectacle that drew jeering crowds was the sight of the women as they left the barbers with their close-cropped hair. Training went on apace and the unit received its special insignia – a red and black arrowhead. Drill and rifle shooting were the main aspects of training which Yashka supervised minutely.

The Battalion of Death had some interesting visitors during their training, including Mrs Emmeline Pankhurst, the British suffragette, who became a regular caller at the barracks, 'watching it with deep concern as it grew into a well-disciplined military unit'. A not so welcome visitor was the revolutionary leader Kerensky, who attempted to get Yashka to disband the battalion, threatening her with a revolver. Fortunately a sentry raised the alarm and all the women, many with their rifles, came to her defence and dispersed her assailants.

After further brushes with the Bolsheviks, she received permission to take her battalion to the front line, but to her dismay found that the situation there was not much better. She seems to have spent her time trying to persuade the unruly soldiers and deserters to follow the example of her women and get on with fighting the real enemy, Germany. She herself was in and out of trouble with the revolutionary regime. The army that she loved had become little more than a savage mob and eventually it was decided to disband her battalion – 'a pitiful finale to an heroic chapter in the history of Russian womanhood'.

In later years Yashka's involvement with the revolution induced her to visit America in an attempt to explain the problems that Russia faced and obtain humanitarian assistance. Isaac Don Levine, who met her during the visit, left a pen picture of this redoubtable woman:

'Like Joan of Arc, Botchkareva is the symbol of her country.... Botchkareva is an astounding typification of peasant Russia with all her virtues and vices. Educated to the extent of being able to scribble her own name with difficulty – she is endowed with the genius of logic. Ignorant of history and literature – the natural lucidity of her mind is such as to lead her directly to the very fundamental truths of life. Religious with all the fervour of her primitive soul – she is tolerant in a fashion befitting a philosopher. Devoted to her country with every fibre of her being – she is free from impassioned partisanship and selfish patriotism. Overflowing with good nature and kindness – she is as yet capable of savage outbursts and brutal acts.... In a word Botchkareva embodies all these paradoxical characteristics of Russian nature that have made Russia a puzzle to the world.'

CHAPTER 10

The Opportunists

James Barry and Dorothy Lawrence, separated by a century, both embarked on army careers, posing as men, but for very different reasons. Dr Barry's opportunism arose from circumstances beyond her control after experiencing the lack of freedom that has dogged women throughout the ages whenever they tried to enter a man's world on anything approaching equal terms. Yet although she succeeded in reaching the top of the tree in a male-dominated profession, the initial decision to embark on such a career must have been taken for her, as she would have been far too young to appreciate the possible outcome.

In the case of Dorothy Lawrence there is the nagging doubt as to whether she acted for patriotic reasons or for the notoriety which her discovery, as a serving soldier, would inevitably bring. Her performance in action seems pathetic by comparison with a true professional like Flora Sandes – perhaps she simply lacked the physique and stamina. If she had genuinely wanted to 'do her bit' towards winning the war, surely she could have enlisted more easily as a nurse or ambulance driver rather than trying by subterfuge to become a soldier – and a not very successful one at that. Opportunist - or mere sensation seeker? The reader must decide.

James Barry, an officer and a gentleman

James Barry's story begins in Scotland where in 1809, at the extremely early age of ten, she was enrolled at Edinburgh University as a literary and medical student. Naturally she was dressed as a boy; although age seems not to have been a bar to entry, sex certainly was. Edinburgh was still refusing to allow women permission to study in medical classes fifty years later – and the first female doctor in Great Britain, Elizabeth Garrett Anderson, did not graduate until the year of James Barry's death.

Secrecy, then, was essential from the very start. It is known that she was accompanied to Edinburgh by her aunt, a Mrs Bulkley, but her parentage is shrouded in mystery. Some early biographers have represented her as the illegitimate daughter of the Prince Regent, others as the daughter or granddaughter of a Scottish earl. She was undoubtably from a good family; indeed, one of her patrons was General Francisco de Miranda, a Venezuelan soldier and scholar who had, incidentally, been the lover of Catherine the Great! Another was David Stuart Erskine, Earl of Buchan. She dedicated her thesis (on hernia of the groin) to both of them and signed her school books James Miranda Stuart Barry.

Despite her tender years and the fact that her thesis had to be argued in Latin before she could graduate, she passed her MD brilliantly. In 1812 she moved to London to continue her studies at St Thomas's Hospital as a 'Pupil Dresser' and apprentice to Sir Astley Cooper, a leading surgeon of the day. Hospitals in those days were vile, filthy places and many students fainted at the sights and smells. The dead bodies they worked on came from the prisons but, like most surgeons of the era, Sir Astley was not above a bit of 'body snatching' when supplies ran out. These were hardly the ideal working conditions for a young man, let alone a girl.

A year later, together with a student friend called Jobson, she went to the army depot at Chatham to apply to join the Army Medical Department. Perhaps her influential friends had persuaded her that this was the life career in which they could be of the greatest help to her. Certainly it would also offer the best chance of her escaping detection, as she could spend most of her service out of England, in a relatively closed society. She passed her exams with flying colours and, at the ripe old age of fourteen, was gazetted as a Hospital Assistant, the most junior officer in the Army Medical Department. She has been described as being slight of build, with high cheekbones, haunted blue eyes and reddish hair. She took to wearing boots with thick soles and medium high heels to make herself look taller. In her scarlet tunic, tight breeches, cocked hat with large feathers, plus sword almost as big as herself, she must have looked a strange and comical figure!

After a short sojourn at the hospital in Plymouth garrison, she was posted to Stoke, and little is known of her for the next two years. In 1816, she was gazetted as Assistant Surgeon to the Forces and posted to the Cape of Good Hope, where yet another of her influential patrons 'just happened to be' Commander in Chief and Governor. This was Lord Charles Somerset, second son of the Duke of Beaufort. His mother owned Stoke Park, a property close to Barry's first posting; and his brother was to become Lord Raglan, who would later exert his influence on the career of the well-connected little doctor.

During her early years in the Cape, James Barry established a reputation as an able, hard-working surgeon, performing some remarkable operations. At one time there was gossip about her pronounced feminine appearance but nevertheless she seems to have carried off the deception. After she had been appointed personal physician to the Governor and his family, she was in a privileged position, as Lord Charles ruled the colony like a paternal dictator. She also appears to have done her damnedest to appear a normal man – immaculately dressed, always in demand at parties and balls, even reputed to be something of a lady-killer! At the same time she wore padded jackets to bolster her tiny figure – the natives called her the 'kapok doctor' – and gave strict orders that no one was ever to enter her bedroom where she slept with her poodle Psyche (a sequence of similarly named poodles appears to have accompanied her throughout her remarkable career). She was also attended by a succession of coloured servants.

Life in the Cape was pleasant enough but, as was to happen everywhere she went, Dr Barry fell foul of the bureaucracy and cupidity of civil servants. The reasons for this were that she detested sham and dishonesty (apart, of course, from her own deception) and always strove to do her very best for the sick, poor and oppressed, speaking out in their defence without a thought for the consequences. She was also very stubborn and possessed a caustic wit and a terrible temper that she found difficult to control. It led her, for example, into fighting a duel with a Captain Cloete, the Governor's aide. They fought a duel with pistols under the oak trees at Alphen, over some disparaging remarks which Barry had made about a Dutch woman visitor. For many years after the duel (neither of the combatants was hurt) there was the inference that it was an 'affair of the heart' and that Barry was herself in love with the gallant captain and objected to his interest in the other woman. Another interpretation is that she appears to have idolised Lord Charles who, despite many arguments and differences of opinion, invariably supported her against his civil servants. To add spice to the mystery is the startling statement made by the woman who laid out James Barry's body after her death – that not only was she a woman but also that she had a child when young. Who could the father have been? The young Dr Jobson with whom she joined the army? Captain Cloete with whom she became firm friends after the duel? Or perhaps someone of even more exalted station – which would account for all the help she received when in difficulty.

Her subsequent army career abroad continued to be varied and eventful. From the Cape she went on to serve all over the world – Mauritius, Jamaica, St Helena, the West Indies, Malta, Corfu and Canada. Everywhere she found sickness, disease and dirt, plus official neglect, corruption and indifferent administration. Everywhere she endeavoured to improve the lot of the sick and ailing, and everywhere she fell foul of the bureaucrats. Inevitably disaster was bound to strike somewhere along the line, when her powerful friends would be unable to help her. It happened in St Helena.

She was court-martialled for 'conduct unbecoming to an officer and a gentleman', after yet another battle with the petty officials who ran the colony. She was rightly acquitted of the wholly unjust charges, but it was a blot on her career. In 1845, a frightening incident took place while she was suffering from a bout of fever – the first time in thirty-two years that she herself had been a patient. Two officers entered her bedroom, despite strict orders that no one was to visit her there. Written accounts indicate that her closely guarded secret was discovered by them. Fortunately she regained sufficient control of herself to make them swear on the Bible to keep her secret so long as she lived – and to their credit this seems to be what they did.

In Corfu she treated a number of sick and wounded from the Crimea and returned with them to the war front to see things for herself. She had previously volunteered for the war but had been refused on the grounds that she was too senior. Dr John Hall went in her stead and it was he, of course, with whom Florence Nightingale crossed swords. She called him 'the Knight of the Crimean Burial Grounds'. Dr Barry met Florence during a visit to the Crimea and clearly did not approve of civilians meddling in army affairs, giving her a good ticking off. Miss Nightingale wrote years later: 'I have never had such a blackguard rating in my life – I who have had more than any woman – than from Barry ... (she) behaved like a brute.' It is a pity that two such dedicated and zealous reformers, who had the same interests at heart, could not have met under happier circumstances, which might have allowed them to work together to improve the lot of the common soldier. Whereas Florence Nightingale became a household name as the heroine of the Crimea, Dr Barry returned to England in 1857, unnoticed, and learned that, after serving more than forty years in warm climes, she was to be posted to Canada. With the death of Lord Raglan two years earlier, all her patrons were apparently gone and for the first time in her career she was without a close friend in high places. After a short leave she obediently went off to face the rigours of her first Canadian winter, with temperatures well below freezing point.

It must have been quite a shock to her system after all those years in the sun but, true to type, she did not let it affect her resolve or her boundless enthusiasm. Muffled in furs, worn over her immaculate uniform frock coat, she was out in all weathers, driving about in a bright red sleigh, which overturned on many an occasion. Renowned for her waspish temper, she is remembered from this period as 'having tiny hands, almost ashen countenance and aquiline features, set off by an unmistakable flaxen wig'.

In 1859, after two years devoted to trying to improve the soldiers' conditions in Canada, travelling many hundreds of miles to inspect hospitals, barracks and camps, she caught influenza and bronchitis so badly that in May she had to come home. Weak and exhausted, she barely survived the journey. In June she attended a medical board which pronounced her unfit for further service and she was placed on half pay, effective from 19 July 1859. Barry herself was far from convinced that her military career should be thus terminated and protested as strongly as she could. She had been made Inspector General of Hospitals in December 1858, had forty-six years of army service behind her and had just reached the peak of her profession. But her protests were in vain; embittered and thoroughly dissatisfied, James Barry went into the obscurity of retirement.

She survived another six years, long enough to see her name in the Army List as the senior of Her Majesty's Inspector Generals of Hospitals, a rank equivalent to that of major-general. Sadly no honours or decorations came her way and she spent her last years travelling abroad to revisit some of the places in which she had served. A fellow traveller during one of these journeys was a Colonel Rogers, who later told, in a book about Barry entitled *A Modern Sphinx*, that he shared a cabin with Barry whilst sailing between St Thomas and Barbados:

> 'I was on the top bunk, she on the lower berth – of course without any suspicion on my part. I well remember how in a harsh and peevish voice she ordered me out of the cabin, blow high, blow low – while she dressed in the mornings. "Now then youngster, clear out of my cabin while I dress," she would say.'

Barry was back in England in 1864 and after spending some time in Cumberland as the guest of the Earl of Lonsdale, returned to London and took up lodgings in a dentist's house in Marylebone. She fell ill during an episode of summer diarrhoea and died on 25 July 1865, one of sixteen victims in the area.

She was buried in Kensal Green Cemetery, the plot costing three guineas, quite a large sum in those days. There is a fascinating report that two imposing footmen called at her lodgings and took away all her belongings, including her poodle Psyche, the last of the line. Her coloured servant had his passage paid back to Jamaica by an unknown benefactor, who still remains unknown. The Irish woman Sophia Bishop, who laid out the body, was outraged. 'The devil a general,' she said, 'it's a woman and a woman who has had a child.' There is a wealth of evidence, and no doubt at all, that the doctor was a woman. In an age when most of her sex were confined to the drawing room and the sewing basket, piano and painting, she not only managed to hold her own in a man's world but did so with panache and with a display of dogged courage and endurance that would have done credit to the toughest male.

Dorothy Lawrence

In her autobiography, Dorothy Lawrence described herself as 'Sapper Dorothy Lawrence, the only English woman soldier, late Royal Engineers,

51st Division, 179th Tunnelling Company, British Expeditionary Forces'. The opening words of her book set a strange scene:

> 'It was midsummer 1915 that an English girl cycled alone into that part of the war zone situated at that time fifteen miles from the firing line near Paris. Any girl cyclist would have looked inharmonious in any possible surroundings except primeval chaos. She was a picture of unloveliness. I am that girl in question; I can make that statement! I rode on a ramshackle cycle, priced originally "£2 a bargain" in a London shop and costing another £3 for its conveyance over the water. From that wonderful home of fashion, Paris, I rode rigged out in an untrimmed felt hat – though sunshine broiled the very pavements – and the shabbiest of clothes, together with the largest brown-paper parcel that ever dangled behind the saddle of any lady's cycle. That overloaded cycle groaned, it joggled and rattled all along the road. At last the mudguard broke; cycle, I and mudguard, all three groaned together. So I arrived.'

Although she would probably have excited little comment in the present free and easy age, bearing in mind that she was living at a time when 'nice girls' did not travel alone, her appearance and method of propulsion must have been cause for considerable comment even on a quiet English country lane. What makes her story all the more extraordinary was the fact that she was in the middle of the war zone, within sight and sound of the guns that had already claimed many victims. In fact, she was calmly trying to get to the front-line trenches. The first place she reached was Creil, which had been the scene of fighting and bore all the marks of war. She found a suitable café to stay at and, being bilingual, had various interesting conversations with French soldiers in the town. But the fact that she was 'une petite Anglaise', and alone in such a place, naturally prompted questions from the *poilus*, which Dorothy must have answered to their satisfaction. She even applied for, and was granted, a safe-conduct pass to visit the Senlis forest, an area that had formerly been within the battle zone.

She cycled on to Senlis, finding it even more ruined than Creil, and after two nights there was told that her pass had expired and that she must leave. Indeed, the local gendarmes were very suspicious of her, reckoning that she must be a spy. One particular policeman kept his eye on her all the time, so she pretended to leave, intending to live rough in the forest. She had brought with her a big white linen bag and she stuffed it full of as many provisions as she could find:

> 'Higgledy-piggledy I put into that bag – spirit lamp, bread, candle, butter, matches, eggs, saucepan, and a bottle of water.... I then tramped away, leaving my cycle hidden under a shed. For several miles I walked. I left Senlis on one of those nights when moonlight dodges darkness....'

Towards midnight she reached the forest and set down under the tall pines: 'Suddenly heavy booms rent the air; guns bellowed – evidently very near at hand. So here I was. Here, under the gunfire, alone at midnight, in this weird forest!' Calmly Dorothy got out her stove, boiled an egg for her supper and then used the water to make cocoa. Very early in the morning, unable to sleep in the continual din, she walked down to the river and tried her luck with a fishing rod that she had bought in Creil. She was joined by a young French officer who gave her useful advice and together they managed to catch half-a-dozen small fish. He did not seem to find it at all odd that a young English woman should be alone, fishing in the forest. That night she found a warmer place to sleep – in a haystack, only to be bitten all over by harvest bugs. As she could not reach the trenches she decided to make her way back to Paris and to try a different approach.

On her return she enlisted help from among the thousands of British soldiers who were thronging Paris. The two soldiers, with 'faces of clean-minded boys', whom she picked up opposite one of the railway stations, assumed initially that she was 'out for love', but when she explained what she wanted, they sportingly offered to help her. What Dorothy was after, of course, was a uniform so that she could pass herself off as a man. Since it was normal for French women to do soldiers' washing, the two privates somehow managed to obtain and smuggle out of their barracks items of a complete uniform, pretending it was laundry:

'Regularly ... I used to meet the men under the trees of a famous boulevard and the "washing" changed hands there.... Surprising how much "linen" can leave one billet from two men in a week! The first wash happened to be a pair of military boots; the second consisted of khaki trousers; whilst the third newspaper parcel to change hands under those trees turned out to be braces, cap, jacket, shirt and puttees. So much for that week's wash! What a lark....'

Putting on and fitting the uniform was not easy – and she could not ask anyone to help her. She resorted to the time-honoured method of disguising her feminine curves with swathes of bandages and padding her back with cotton wool. The result was a thick-set, plumpish, manly figure topped by a rather small head and boyish face which she really could not disguise.

It is clear that the two soldiers agreed to help Dorothy in the conviction that she would never be able to get near enough to the front line to be in any danger. They let her walk about with them in uniform, teaching her elementary drill in the side streets of Paris, so at least she could know how to salute and march. They also helped her to forge a leave pass, telling her what to write. She tried unsuccessfully to get hold of a paybook but did at least acquire an identity disc which read, D. Smith 175331, 1st Leicester Regt. RC – the last two letters standing for Roman Catholic, which was not her persuasion – and this she wore around her neck.

Her accomplices advised her to make for Béthune, from where she would be able to reach the trenches fairly easily, though clearly they did not consider it possible for her to get there. However, they had reckoned without Dorothy's determination and ingenuity. Reporting to a local *mairie*, she explained that she would like a safe-conduct pass to Calais and that she wanted to go by bicycle rather than train. He seemed perfectly happy about this and even when she casually mentioned that she would like to go via Amiens and Béthune to visit friends, he obediently wrote 'Béthune' on the pass, obviously forgetting that it was near the front line. She now had the means of achieving her goal.

The *patron* of her boarding house, who had been let in on her secret, helped her to pack everything into a large brown-paper parcel, which

142

Dorothy tied to the back of her old bicycle, and then rode into Paris to catch the train for the first leg of her journey. Before boarding the train she had one final thing to do – to get a regulation military haircut. At St Lazare station she found just the person to do the job and after much persuasion he cut off her long hair. He may not have been a professional hairdresser because she wrote: 'Five minutes later I looked in the glass. Well, I won't say what I looked like! He had cut close to my head in true outline of a British private....'

The next day she was off. What a strange figure she must have been, with a deliberately dirty face, short hair, white linen hat pulled down over her eyes and pushing her ramshackle, heavily laden bike. She arrived in Amiens and after a brush with a suspicious gendarme on the steps of the cathedral, decided to leave straight away and headed towards Albert, then the forward area of the right-hand sector of the British-held portion of the front line, only a few hundred yards away from the German trenches.

Now dressed in her uniform, Dorothy joined the crowds on the road to Albert – refugees going one way and soldiers the other, as well as military vehicles of all types heading for the front. She was stopped by various sentries but none of them held her for long. After a night in Albert she set off on her bike, towards the trenches, chatting with many of the Scottish soldiers she passed along the way. Seeing how big and brawny they were, she realised that she could not join their battalion. Suddenly she spotted a soldier who was more of her height among this throng of towering, kilted Scotsmen. He turned out to be a sapper – one Thomas Dunn from Lancashire – who was to be her firmest and most helpful friend. Convinced that he would never be able to talk her out of what she wanted to do, he helped her to obtain a Royal Engineers cap badge. Together they hunted for a suitable hiding place for Dorothy until such time as she could join his unit. They chose a row of deserted cottages on the outskirts of Albert:

'In front lay the trenches, approached by a small cabbage plot; at the rear of Albert's statue of the Virgin balanced in mid-air, brooding over the place; and immediately below these cottages cellar dug-outs offered ready shelter. Into one of these dug-outs I plunged, pulling in that precious cycle...'

143

Tommy Dunn then went off, promising to get back as soon as he could and she was left alone for days and nights before he managed to return. 'Tonight I go on night shift and you can come too,' he said, '... after dusk we will creep along to the courtyard, mingle with the crowd and line up when they do.' All went well and some hours later an excited Dorothy was marching off with the file of sappers; her army service had really begun.

After ten days and nights spent under incessant fire, Dorothy came to recognise that she would not be able to keep up her pretence for much longer - on practical grounds as well as the fact that she was racked with rheumatic pains, dizzy with lack of food and exposure to the elements, and already seriously weakened from two months of trying to get to the front; she decided that she had had enough and must tell someone in authority – the only snag being that she did not want to get those who had helped her into trouble. She burnt all her papers except her passport and safe-conduct passes and told Tommy to inform his sergeant that there was a girl in the ranks.

The sergeant was pleasant and affable but placed her under arrest. Dorothy was highly indignant but in her heart of hearts must have known that she would not be allowed to stay. She had regained her composure when she was taken in front of the colonel to be questioned. He was a perfect gentleman, not only finding her comfortable quarters but also locking the door 'for her own safety' before leaving her that night.

So began her long and involved period of arrest and cross-questioning – she was passed from the colonel to division, division to army, where she was questioned by three generals, all suspecting that she was a spy. Even when it became obvious that she was not, they were still unsure what to do with her – so they confined her in the Convent of St Omer. Then, on the personal orders of the Commander in Chief, Sir John French, she was released. Under guard she was taken to Boulogne and remained in custody until she was shipped out. Landing in Folke-stone, she was interviewed by an officer who listened politely to all she had to say and then made her promise not to speak about it to anyone until given official permission. So, if Dorothy had any ideas of selling her story to the newspapers, and from some of her remarks that seems to have been her idea, 'for the sake of my country', she very reluctantly agreed to say nothing.

So ended the military career of Sapper Dorothy Lawrence. She had certainly achieved part of what she set out to do, namely in getting to the trenches and serving as a soldier. One cannot help but feel, however, that she was more than a little put out by the fact that the army had not allowed her to become a heroine and had packed her off home without so much as a pat on the back or a 'well done'. How bitterly disappointed she must have been.

CHAPTER 11

Spies

Probably the first people to use spies were the Chinese – reputedly from the fifth century BC, when the philosopher Mo Tzu (who wrote a book on the subject) promoted the idea of reporting to those in authority anyone who did evil deeds, thus pre-dating the papal-inspired Inquisition by several hundreds of years. The Bible, too, contains many references to spies – the best known being Delilah, a paid agent of the Philistines, who discovered the secret of Samson's strength and then used her knowledge to weaken him so that the Philistines could take him prisoner. The Romans sent out spies days before advancing on their enemies and waited until the intelligence reports had been gathered before making their final plans.

The medieval Church – and the Pope in particular – had by far the greatest espionage system of the so-called Dark Ages, the Inquisition of course being its most infamous weapon. In England Cardinal Wolsey, and in France Cardinal Richelieu, had their own spy networks – the latter additionally immortalised by many adventure spy books as the archetypal villain – and used women as well as men as agents.

In 1573 Sir Francis Walsingham was appointed by Queen Elizabeth I as Secretary of State. He was a fanatical Protestant and an expert in diplomacy and espionage. In the seventeen years he served his queen he built up an impressive secret service, reputed to consist of more than fifty spies in Europe and at home, as well as a great many secret contacts. He also used women as spies, believing that they were perfectly placed for the job. When he died there was no one to take his place and presumably his secret service gradually petered out. It was resuscitated, however, by Oliver Cromwell when he came to power and Pepys wrote that Cromwell spent '£70,000 annually for intelligence'. Whether any of these spies were actually women is unrecorded but it is more than probable that maids and other female servants were employed, as they could, and did, certainly 'overhear' many private conversations.

Chevalier d'Eon

At Carlton House on Easter Monday 1787, the Prince of Wales entertained his guests to an amazing fencing display. The principal duellist was the Chevalier de Saint Georges, a young man from Guadaloupe who had come to England after years in the service of the Duke of Orléans, in order to enhance his name as a swordsman. He was reputed to be one of the finest in the world so naturally his opponents were carefully selected. It was therefore quite a surprise for the eager audience to discover that the figure emerging to do battle with Saint Georges was short, stout, nearly sixty years of age and dressed in women's clothes! Mrs Fitzherbert and her fashionable friends must have had quite a laugh at the prince's apparently bizarre attempt to amuse them. To quote a contemporary account: 'Though encumbered with three petticoats, she not only parried all the thrusts of her powerful antagonist but even touched him by what is termed a coupe de temps, which all his dexterity could not ward off.' Afterwards Saint-Georges admitted that his unlikely looking opponent had actually hit him no less than seven times! The Prince of Wales personally congratulated the victor and presented her with a pair of splendid duelling pistols as a memento of the occasion.

The name of this strange little person was the Chevalier d'Eon de Beaumont, who was born on 5 October 1727, of an old French family of the minor nobility, at Tonnerre in Burgundy. She was originally baptised Charles Geneviève Louise Auguste André Timothée – but it has been said that at the age of three she was publicly dedicated to the Virgin Mary under the names Charlotte Geneviève Louise Augusta Timothea, to which the name Maria was added by the Archbishop of Seurre, when he confirmed the child. This confusion over names highlights the problem that was to remain with the unfortunate d'Eon all through her life.

Until the age of seven she apparently wore girl's clothes but her education from that date was that of a boy. She studied hard, first at school in Paris and then at the age of twelve at the Collège Mazarin, obtaining a law degree in August 1748. In those days she was described as being 'small and slight in build, with a high-pitched voice, delicately cut features and singularly smooth skin which emphasised the beardlessness of his face'. D'Eon probably intended to practise law; however, the unexpected death of her father in 1749 left her in reduced circumstances, but she was rescued by the help of influential friends, some of whom employed the young d'Eon as secretary.

In 1755, while in the service of the Prince de Conti, d'Eon was sent to the Russian court at St Petersburg as a secret agent of the French king Louis XV. Here she resumed female attire and although details of her mission are not clear, she may have been employed as a 'reader' to the Empress Elizabeth. In later years at least one member of the Russian royal family, Princess Dashkov, said that she remembered d'Eon in St Petersburg as a woman. D'Eon returned to France the following year carrying a secret letter from the Empress to King Louis – together with her agreement to receive an official French representative. D'Eon thus played a part in bringing Russia into the Austro–Franco alliance which had been reformed in 1756, in answer to Prussia's alliance with England. She received 300 ducats and a miniature of the Empress for her hard work and was shortly sent back to Russia as an attaché at the legation, but still engaged in espionage.

In 1757 d'Eon was employed on a similar mission carrying letters from the Empress to Louis and Maria Theresa. She was in Vienna when news of the battle of Prague arrived and she was sent immediately to carry to Versailles the important news of the Prussian invasion of Bohemia. En route the coach overturned and d'Eon's leg was broken. Pausing only to have it set, she continued her journey, reaching Paris thirty-six hours ahead of the special messenger sent by the Austrian ambassador. This time her zeal was rewarded by the personal congratulations of the king, the presentation of a gold and pearl snuff box bearing Louis's portrait, and a commission as a lieutenant of dragoons. Louis even sent one of his own surgeons to attend to the broken leg but despite this d'Eon was forced to remain in bed for three months.

In September 1762 d'Eon accompanied the Duc de Nivernais when he was sent to London to arrange details of the peace which was designed to end the Anglo-French part of the Seven Years War. The treaty was ratified in Paris the following February and once again d'Eon received just rewards for all the work she had put in – indeed the duke had written of her: 'D'Eon works from morning to night; I cannot tell you his zeal, his vigilance, his activity ... his discretion....' In addition to a handsome gratuity (which arrived in the nick of time as d'Eon was deep in debt) the king conferred the rank of chevalier upon her, which entitled her to wear the Cross of St Louis. Returning to England, she was made a minister plenipotentiary and was at the very height of her diplomatic career – only one step away from becoming a fully fledged ambassador.

'How are the mighty fallen' – unfortunately d'Eon seems to have let this newly acquired importance to go to her head. When the new ambassador, Comte de Cuerchy, arrived, she refused to obey his orders and demanded that all the considerable private debts she had run up be paid by him. In addition, she refused to give up certain compromising letters and papers with which she had been entrusted and flatly refused to go back to Paris unless her orders of recall had been signed by the king himself. There is some excuse for all this, for she had received a secret letter from the king which ordered her to resume female dress, withdraw from public notice, but remain in England and retain all secret correspondence, to ensure that it did not fall into the wrong hands. D'Eon obeyed some of these royal commands but refused to adopt female clothing, nor did she withdraw from public life. Instead she started a vitriolic verbal battle with de Cuerchy, which culminated in swearing publicly that he had bribed someone to murder her. The scandal became even more public when d'Eon challenged de Cuerchy to settle their differences 'by a force of arms, as becomes two soldiers'. De Cuerchy refused, replying that a general would not fight a mere captain of dragoons. This so incensed d'Eon that she was even more determined to be avenged, and on 12 February 1765 de Cuerchy found himself indicted before the grand jury of Middlesex for attempted murder. Although the court found him guilty they had no jurisdiction because of his diplomatic status and the case was quashed. However, the mob following the case came out strongly in favour of d'Eon, attacked de Cuerchy in the street, attempted to lynch him and smashed all the windows in his house and chapel. De Cuerchy wisely decided to take some leave in France, leaving d'Eon victorious.

France's embarrassment over this quarrel between her diplomatic representatives was far from over and the Comte de Broglie was sent to visit d'Eon in order to repossess the secret correspondence, making various offers, including that of a large pension. He was partly successful but the bargaining dragged on until the death of Louis in May 1774. Then, with the full revelation of the secret correspondence in which d'Eon had been involved, the hard bargaining began. D'Eon finally agreed to return every-thing for a yearly pension of 12,000 livres and the right to return to France. The bargain also included the undertaking that she would seek no further quarrel with de Cuerchy, either private or through the courts, and finally that henceforth she would only wear women's clothing.

On 13 August 1777 d'Eon left London and a few days later arrived at Versailles, dressed not as a woman but as a captain of dragoons. This produced the order for d'Eon to 'resume the garments of her sex' and forbade her 'to appear in any part of the kingdom, in any other garments than those proper for a woman'. It took two months for the necessary dresses to be made and then the transformation took place under the watchful eye of the royal ladies in waiting:

'She ... d'Eon ... was anointed with fragrant perfumes, her hair was curled and a magnificent headdress put on her; her gown, petticoats and stockings were of the richest materials and she was adorned with bracelets, a necklace, earrings and rings....
In this quality she was presented at court and there compelled to remain two years, that she might become moulded into her new condition.'

When war with England broke out in 1778, and France allied herself with the American colonists against Britain, d'Eon asked to be allowed to resume masculine dress and to serve as a volunteer in the navy; but she was refused and went back to live with her mother in Tonnerre, where she remained for the next six years.

In 1785, two years after the Treaty of Versailles had ended the War of American Independence, d'Eon went back to England where she had many friends. The French Revolution of 1792 put an end to her pension and the only means she had left to support herself was to give fencing exhibitions, such as the one already mentioned. In August 1796 she was badly wounded in the armpit by a foil that had lost its button; the wound was about four inches long and very painful and she was by this time sixty-eight years old. She never recovered from the injury, being confined to the house for the remaining years of her life. She was supported by the charity of her friends and the sale of her private possessions, living quietly with a Mrs Mary Cole, the widow of a naval inventor.

She died on 21 May 1810 and the certificate made out by the surgeon who did the post-mortem examination stated that the body had many feminine characteristics ... breasts remarkably full, arms, hands and fingers those of a stout woman; legs and feet corresponding with the arms. But he reported the sexual organs to be male and perfectly formed – a shock for Mrs Cole, who had never for one moment doubted that her companion was a woman.

D'Eon was buried in the churchyard of St Pancras and the grave has since disappeared – swept away during the expansion of the Midland Railway lines in that area. However, the Baroness Burdett-Coutts, a Victorian philanthropist, paid for a monument to be erected in the churchyard, which bears the names of those whose graves were destroyed.

Transvestite, hermaphrodite, homosexual – d'Eon has been described as all of these both during her lifetime and since, by her various biographers. If she had been fortunate enough to live in our enlightened age, she would have been the perfect candidate for a sex change operation because she was so clearly, at heart, a woman. Perhaps she should be allowed the last word: 'If the Great Master of the universe has not endowed us with all the external vigour of manhood, he has amply made amends by gifting my head and my heart. I am what the hands of God have made me; satisfied with my weakness.'

Mata Hari

In subsequent generations there were doubtless many women who were employed as spies but nothing is known of them. The first female agent to achieve notoriety was Mata Hari. Born in Leeuwarden, Holland in 1876, and christened Margaretha Geertruida Zelle, she was the daughter of a prosperous hatter and had a good education. After attending a teacher's college in Leiden she married Captain Campbell MacLeod – an officer in the Dutch colonial army – and went with him when he was posted to Java and Sumatra. When they returned to Europe, however, they separated and she made her living by dancing professionally in Paris under the name Lady MacLeod. She soon changed her name to Mata Hari – a Malay term meaning 'eye of the day.'

Attractive in a dark, exotic way, and perfectly happy to appear – scantily clad – performing East Indian-style dances, she was an instant success in Paris and other large cities. She is also reputed to have had many lovers, some of whom were officers in various armies.

Nothing is known of her actual espionage activities. She is reputed to have spied for the French in Belgium and for the Germans in France, and to have had some strange idea of getting Ernest Augustus, Duke of Brunswick-Luneburg (and heir to the dukedom of Cumberland in Britain), to aid the Allies. The British warned the French authorities that she had been spying for the Germans and they kept a close watch on her and eventually arrested her. Mata Hari was tried by a military court in 1917, sentenced and shot by firing squad. Whatever the truth, her name has become synonymous for a seductive female spy.

Edith Louisa Cavell

Edith Cavell was an English nurse who became a heroine in the First World War and was shot by the Germans as a spy in 1915 – despite the efforts of the American and Spanish ministers – causing the rest of the world to consider this act an outrage. She was matron of a hospital in Brussels when Belgium was occupied by the Germans and was subsequently involved with the underground group formed to help British, French and Belgian soldiers to reach the neutral zone of the Netherlands. Over 200 men had escaped capture when Edith Cavell was herself arrested, with others, court martialled and executed as a spy – which has been emphatically repudiated by the British authorities.

Marie-Madeleine Fourcade

There were far more female spies during the Second World War, many of whom were active in the European resistance movements, especially in France.

Noah's Ark was the name given to a large intelligence network founded by Georges Loustaunau-Lacau who was arrested in May 1941; his place was taken by his secretary Marie-Madeleine Fourcade. She was instrumental in re-establishing the link with Secret Intelligence Service (SIS) and by 1943 she had a network of 3000 members, both men and women, operating twenty wireless transmitters. This network was known in London as

Alliance, but Marie-Madeleine chose to give her agents the names of animals or birds and the whole network was thus known as Noah's Ark. In July 1943, after many daring and dangerous escapades, she was persuaded to be airlifted out of France as the Germans were getting too close to her. Out of the 3000 members of the network, 500 died in German hands but they provided information about German defences and order of battle, sending large quantities of information that was picked up by light aircraft, being too much to send by radio. After the war she was a staunch supporter of General de Gaulle and later became a member of the European Parliament. She wrote her autobiography, calling it *Noah's Ark*, and died in 1989.

Christine Granville, GM, OBE, Croix de Guerre

In spite of the English name, Christine was born in Poland. Her father – Count Jerzy Skarbek – was from an ancient and aristocratic Polish family, but he was rather profligate and so had to choose a wife from a wealthy family to ensure that he continued to live in the manner to which he had always been accustomed. He married Stephanie Goldfeder, daughter of a wealthy Jewish banker. Their second child was a daughter Krystyna (Christine) who was born in 1915, and from the start she was the apple of her father's eye. She had an idyllic childhood on the family estate and was a great tomboy in spite of being rather small-boned and fragile. An avid reader of Polish history, and gripped imaginatively by the almost fairy-tale quality of it all, she grew up to be passionately patriotic. She was a very accomplished horsewoman and spent every spare moment, as a teenager, in or around the stables.

In 1930 her handsome, much loved father died, at a time when the Goldfeder fortune was near to collapse. There was just enough money for her mother to live on. At eighteen Christine had a brief marriage – to Charles Getlich, from a German-Polish family – but was soon divorced.

In 1938 she married Jerzy Gizycki, a Ukrainian writer. He was a restless man and they travelled all over Europe where they were on friendly terms with many diplomats. Later he was his country's consul in Addis Ababa. When the Germans invaded Poland in 1939 the Gizyckis returned to Europe and settled in London, anxious to find a way of helping Poland and its people. Christine was also very worried about her mother who was still living in Warsaw.

Not long after their arrival Christine was introduced to Sir Robert Vansittart at the Foreign and Commonwealth Office. She told him of her plan to go to Budapest to produce propaganda leaflets and then distribute them in Poland to keep the spirit of resistance alive. She planned to get into Poland through the Tatra Mountains – she was an excellent skier – and she was known to the local guides. After consideration, her plan was accepted and a cover story – as a British journalist collecting items for articles in magazines – was created for her. She left England on 21 December 1939, for Budapest.

When the Germans marched into Poland, thousands of Polish officers, soldiers and civilians escaped across the border into Hungary. Army personnel were put into internment camps. A new, hastily formed Polish government based in France organised official cells in Hungary and Romania in order to help the floods of refugees who had fled ahead of the Germans, particularly into Hungary. It was easy for Christine to find friends in Budapest who would help her to get back into Poland.

It was during this period in Budapest that she met, and fell in love with, a fellow Pole – Andrew Kowerski. He had been a member of the only Polish motorised brigade, called the Black Brigade (because of the colour of their jackets), which had fought the Germans again and again before being beaten, and escaping into Hungary. It was customary, by International Law, for officers and soldiers to be interned, but although Andrew had been detained he had managed to escape. A very resourceful and brave man, he had already won the Virtuti Militari (the Polish Victoria Cross). At the age of twenty-four he had lost a leg in a skiing accident when caught in an avalanche and was extremely lucky to survive. Undeterred by this handicap, after his escape from internment camp he set about helping other soldiers to reach France in order to rejoin the Polish army, which had been rebuilt by General Wladyslaw Sikorski.

Christine and Andrew began to live together but did not allow their affair to interrupt their work. They became very friendly with the British ambassador, Sir Owen O'Malley, his wife Ann Bridge, who was a well-known traveller and writer, and their eighteen-year-old daughter Kate, who immediately formed a crush on Andrew, to her father's embarrassment. A regular escape route for British POWs in Polish camps was formed between Sir Owen and Christine, which involved the Polish underground, to help to get the POWs to Athens and then back to Britain.

Christine did several risky and dangerous journeys through the hazardous Tatra Mountains into Poland, both to distribute her propaganda leaflets and to bring out information to pass on to the British. She also tried desperately to get her mother out of Warsaw but she adamantly refused to leave her home. Later, when back in Budapest, Christine heard that her mother had been taken by the Nazis and she was never heard of again.

Finally it got too dangerous for all concerned, the rescuers and the escapers. On her last journey into Poland Christine had been in bad health. She had caught influenza which left her weak and exhausted and forced her into bed for two weeks when it was discovered that she was coughing blood. Three months later, Andrew and Christine were arrested and questioned for hours by the Gestapo. They were released on the intervention of a local doctor, who sympathised with them, declaring that Christine was very ill.

They realised that they were now going to find life very difficult as the Germans had decided to follow them, only waiting for one slip that would prove that they were spies and allow them to be rearrested. It was definitely time to leave Budapest. They contacted the O'Malleys who gave them British passports and visas (despite their not being able to speak a word of English), and under new names – Christine Granville and Andrew Kennedy – they managed to get into Yugoslavia. From Belgrade they travelled, in their small Opel car, with some microfilms that Christine had been asked to deliver to the British Legation, to Istanbul, and thence through Syria to Cairo.

Christine became a member of Special Operations Executive (SOE), trained in Algiers and was parachuted into occupied France with a new identity – Pauline Armand. Her bravery was legendary; from the horrors of the battle of the Vercors to the rescue of her leader, 'Roger', and two other companions from the prison at Digne, she showed a total disregard for any personal danger. After the D-Day landings, she and 'Roger' set off to find the Allied HQ to offer their services, but by now there was little for them to do. Soon afterwards, realising that their work as agents was over, the team said goodbye and Christine returned to London.

She now discovered that Andrew was in Italy; he too had had many dangerous and daring adventures, and she was eager to see him again. Christine arrived in Bari in the worst winter weather for almost half a century but after the first joy of meeting again they both realised that although they would always remain friends, the romance had gone out of their relationship.

In January 1945 Christine was awarded the George Medal for having saved the lives of two British officers, and later the OBE. The French awarded her the Croix de Guerre with Etoile d'Argent for saving the life of Major Sorenson. She was desperate to get back to Poland and hearing that one of her great friends was posted to the British Embassy in Warsaw, wrote to him to see if he could get her a job there; however, the request was denied.

She was demobbed in May 1945 with a gratuity of £100, small recompense for all her extraordinary deeds in hazardous conditions. The SOE gave her no recognition and neither did her beloved Poland for whom she would willingly have died. She became a naturalised British citizen and took a variety of mundane jobs but, unable to settle, she travelled to see friends in Kenya and then in 1951 sailed to Australia on the maiden voyage of the *Rauhine*, as a stewardess. On the same ship was a steward named Dennis George Muldowney who fell obsessively in love with Christine. He was a solitary and lonely man and Christine took pity on him; when they landed in Australia she tried to introduce him to her friends but they disliked him and virtually ignored him.

Christine was to regret her charitable behaviour towards Muldowney because she was unable to get rid of him; he followed her everywhere, even waiting outside shops while she was with her friends, displaying fits of jealous rage. She did two more journeys to Australia on the same ship and each time experienced the same problems; finally she realised that in order to shake off Muldowney she would have to go somewhere where he could not find her. She wrote to Andrew to tell him of her plan and when she docked in London she went to do her packing before leaving for an 'unknown' destination. Having said goodbye to various Polish friends, she went back to her hotel to finish off her packing only to find Muldowney there. He lunged at her with a long-bladed knife and while a hotel guest phoned for an ambulance and a porter tried to support her head, he stood immobile, saying over and over again, 'I killed her because I loved her.' When the ambulance arrived Christine was dead.

Needless to say, her friends, especially Andrew, who flew in from Bonn, were in a state of complete shock. Having survived all her dangerous exploits during the war, intrepid Christine had died at the hand of an unbalanced, obsessive misfit. The papers, unwilling to believe that their heroine had been murdered, suggested that the former British secret agent had been killed by the Communists or had been done to death by French traitors. Muldowney, nevertheless, was tried, pronounced guilty and hanged on 30 September 1952.

Yvonne Claire Cerneau – 'Jacqueline'

Yvonne Claire Cerneau was born in January 1897 at Maisons-Laffitte, twenty kilometres from Paris. She was the youngest of ten children, most of whom died in infancy. Her father was a horse dealer who bought horses for the French army and took his daughter with him when he went on buying trips. Yvonne's mother was a strong-willed woman who, although she loved her daughter, believed in obedience and discipline. To improve her deportment, she made Yvonne sit for long periods bolt upright on a stool, with a ruler down her back, with a box of buttons to play with to relieve the tedium! This sitting still was to serve her in good stead in later years, as were her contacts in the French army.

After her father died, finding it impossible to live with her domineering mother, Yvonne went to London and got a job at the Galeries Lafayette, a French-owned chain store in Regent Street. She was an attractive eighteen-year-old, small and slight, with dark curly hair, and a lively personality. In 1920 she met and married a waiter from the Piccadilly Hotel, Alex Rudellat, a man nine years older than she was, who had once been an undercover agent. In 1922 she had a baby who was christened Constance Jacqueline; and when the child was seven, her father and mother separated, and she spent time alternately with both of them.

In 1939, ten days after the declaration of war, Constance joined the Auxiliary Territorial Service (ATS). She considered herself as wholly British in spite of her French-Italian parentage. By Christmas that same year she was married – to a sergeant in the Pay Corps named Ronald Pepper. Yvonne liked her new son-in-law and he admired her immensely. Yvonne tried many times to follow her daughter into the ATS but was always turned down because of her age. Her greatest desire was to 'go and do something useful for France'.

In 1942 she got her wish and was finally selected to train for the SOE. No woman had ever been selected as a leader although many were very good at their jobs. After months of training, on 18 July 1942, Yvonne Rudellat left England for Gibraltar and thence, by boat, to France, in appalling weather conditions, the first female member of SOE to be sent abroad. Her code-name during her operations in France was Jacqueline Gautier. Together with Pierre Culioli, she set up and controlled a resistance group around the châteaux of the Loire. After many successful operations both Pierre and Jacqueline were captured by the Germans. While trying to escape arrest by car, Jacqueline was hit in the back of the head by a bullet. Seeing blood oozing from her head, Pierre thought she was dead and, unwilling to be caught, decided to kill himself. So he stepped on the accelerator and closed his eyes. The car crossed a ditch and crashed into the side of a cottage, leaving Pierrre stunned but alive.

Jacqueline was taken to the hospital at Blois where the doctor examining her said that the bullet had stopped short of penetrating the brain and that although her memory might be impaired it was best to leave the bullet where it was for the time being. She was later taken to Ravensbruck concentration camp. On the same transport was another SOE agent – likewise a resistance heroine, Odette Sansom – but they did not meet or know each other. (Violette Szabo was also sent there.) Out of 8000 Frenchwomen in prison camps in Germany only 800 returned to France. Towards the end of February 1945, 2500 elderly and ill women were sent from Ravensbruck to a 'convalescent camp' – Jacqueline was one of them. The name of the camp was Belsen.

In Belsen Jacqueline became ill and gradually deteriorated. By the time that the camp was liberated she was barely alive. She died on either 23 or 24 April 1945 and was buried in one of the death camp's anonymous mass graves.

CHAPTER 12

To Fight or Not to Fight

As already mentioned, there are countless examples of individual women throughout history who, for personal reasons or from necessity, have played a major part in battle. But, in a broader context, the dilemma as to whether or not women should serve in the armed forces and, if so, whether they should be armed and take part in actual military combat, is undoubtedly a twentieth-century problem. In fact, it was only towards the end of the nineteenth century that women began to play a formal part in the treatment of wounded servicemen, let alone engage in a combat role on the battlefield.

British servicewomen

In Great Britain there was never a mention of women serving officially in the army, prior to the First World War. However, in December 1916, the War Office detailed a Lieutenant General Lawson to look into the number and physical categories of soldiers in France, who were not actually in the fighting area, to see whether their tasks could be carried out by women.

In his report, submitted a month later, Lawson recommended that in view of the active part women were already playing in the country's war effort, both at home and overseas, in such vital professions as nursing, they should also be employed in the army in France. There were many dissenting voices, including the CinC in the field – Douglas Haig – who raised such objections as the fact that some women storekeepers would be unable to supervise the trying on of uniforms, or that women would not be strong enough to lift carcasses of beef, if they were employed as butchers! Even Lord Derby, the then Secretary of War, who supported the proposal in principle, had his reservations about complete equality in view of what might happen to women if they were unfortunate enough to be taken prisoner. Despite these well-intentioned but ridiculous arguments, the Women's Army

Auxiliary Corps officially came into existence in July 1917. In April 1918 it changed its title to Queen Mary's Army Auxiliary Corps (QMAAC) and by the end of the war its numbers rose to 40,850. The women were employed in a wide variety of administrative tasks but none of the jobs they performed required them actually to fight in battle. Two years later, on 1 May 1920, the QMAAC was officially disbanded.

War scares in 1938 resulted in the Imperial Defence Committee changing its collective mind about not recruiting women, and on 9 September 1938, a Royal Warrant brought the Auxiliary Territorial Service (ATS) into being. Particularly active members of the ATS of the Second World War were those who served with Anti-Aircraft Command in the mixed AA regiments, who were described by their CinC, General Sir Frederick Pile, as being: 'the first to take their place in a combatant role in any army in the world' – a claim that would have been contested, however, by women snipers and tank commanders of the Soviet Union. The Germans also had 'Flak' girls but they were not introduced until later in the war. The Americans never employed their Women's Army Corps (WAC) in this way and were most intrigued by the British 'Co-ed Gun Girls', as they called them. Members of the ATS operated predictors, height finders and radar sets, in addition to carrying out the more mundane but equally vital tasks of driving, clerking, cooking, etc, thus releasing the men for actual battle duty.

After the war, on 1 February 1949, the ATS changed its name to the Women's Royal Army Corps (WRAC) but otherwise remained unaltered, WRAC units carrying out many tasks but always as sub-units 'blistered' on to a particular unit or establishment, with their own officers and NCOs all wearing the same WRAC cap-badge and with strictly segregated living quarters. It was not until the White Paper of 1980 that the possibility of arming the three women's services, specifically for their own defence, was included. This gave rise to a storm of public protest in the media, despite the fact that many of Britain's NATO allies – USA, Belgium, Canada, Denmark and the Netherlands – had already successfully cleared this emotive hurdle.

The next change followed logically and without the same display of public emotion although its importance was far greater. On 6 April 1992 the WRAC was disbanded and its women soldiers dispersed throughout the army, many into newly formed mixed-sex units, such as the Adjutant General's Corps. In this way many of the barriers that prevented male and female soldiers from doing the same jobs and being treated as equals were swept away overnight.

The debate as to whether or not women should be allowed to go 'all the way' – i.e. eligible for full combat service – has nevertheless continued to rage. In late 1995, after a series of gruelling tests carried out at the MOD research agency at Farnborough, it was decided that women could perform all required military roles with complete success. The programme included route marches in full battle gear, lifting heavy weights, endurance tests and treadmills, etc. Mixed groups of men and women put more effort into the tasks. No final decision has yet been made, so, for the present, only Britain, Greece and Portugal, among European armies, still operate an official ban on women in the front line. How long this will take to change is anyone's guess but the logic is inescapable; the first British woman combat soldier will almost certainly be seen before the end of the century – and she will have to be prepared to shoot in anger at the enemy. A report from the recent Balkans War, for example, told of how, when a Danish tank in the NATO force was fired on by the Bosnian Serbs, the female gunner fired seventy-two rounds in return, stopping only when her ammunition bays were empty. Shall we see mixed British Armoured Fighting Vehicles (AFV) crews in the future, with male and female infantry soldiers sharing the same slit-trench/pup-tent? Very probably.

American servicewomen

Although its early military history closely resembled that of the UK, the American army's problems were on a much more massive scale – there being nearly 100,000 women serving in the WACs alone at the peak of the Second World War. On 14 May 1942 President Roosevelt had signed the bill establishing the Women's Auxiliary Army Corps (WAAC), with an initial authorised strength of 25,000. However, just six moths later, the WAAC had so fully justified its existence that its authorised strength was greatly increased and an intensive recruiting programme started.

The first WAAC training centre had opened at Fort Des Moines, Iowa on 20 July 1942, running four-week courses for auxiliaries (six weeks for officer candidates). The 'Pallas Athene' cap-badge soon became well known throughout the US Army as the women began their jobs as clerks, cooks, drivers, radio operators, radio repair technicians and the like. A little more than a year later there were some 65,000 women serving in over 240 camps and stations around the USA and abroad, coping with 155 different types of job. On 30 September 1943 the WAAC ceased to exist and the Women's Army Corps (WAC) came into being. A survey taken in May 1943 showed that 40.9% were under twenty-five and that 70% were single; 64.4% were in offices and administration; 5.6% technical and professional; 2.7% in communications; 2.7% in mechanical, trade and manual; 2.7% in supply and stock; and 1.8% radio.

No WAC served in Korea and only one WAC unit (of about 125) went to Vietnam after 1967. Since 1971, however, the change has been phenomenal. The separate WAC is no more, women being totally integrated into all military trades and employments. To quote from an article in the *Army Magazine* of February 1978:

> 'Men and women scrub their "co-ed" barracks knee to knee; sweat together during morning physical training; gripe together during many a greasy, sweaty task. Female sergeants command male privates. Female officers command platoons. As staff officers, they no longer perform just as personnel officers, they now work in intelligence and operations.'

What caused this dramatic change was the realisation that an all-regular army could not afford to pass up the recruiting potential which was presented every year by over 300,000 young women in their late teens, who were well able to meet the stringent US army entry standards. By 1978 there were 50,000 women soldiers and this figure has been steadily rising. They take the basic, advanced, individual and officers' candidate training alongside men. (In 1995, after a great deal of publicity, a court ruled that a woman should be allowed to enter West Point, but she later withdrew as she could not maintain the necessary fitness levels rather than being unable to cope with the 'hazing' that takes place in 'plebe' year). Women get the same pay, serve the same overseas tours and receive the same benefits and retirement pensions as men. They all must prove their proficiency with the M16 rifle, the grenade launcher, Claymore mine, M60 machine gun and certain light anti-tank weapons.

Complete integration, of course, is not without its problems and in the late 1990s there have been numerous cases of harassment of women in the military, some of which have ended in sexual assault, rape and even murder. In December 1996 *Time Magazine* included an article which claimed that the experiment with sexually integrated military had probably failed and that it was time to change to an all-female military. Whilst this was no doubt meant humorously, there is still a serious underlying problem which, so far, refuses to go away.

Women soldiers worldwide

A review of the rest of the world shows that several armies have had women soldiers serving in the front line for many years. Apart from the already cited example from the Russian Revolution period – the aptly named 'Women's Battalion of Death' organised in Russia in May 1917 by Yashka Botchkareva, who had herself served throughout the war in an otherwise all-male infantry battalion – Russian women also served in combat units in the Second World War, commanding tanks, acting as infantry snipers, etc, and receiving awards for bravery. A conservative estimate put the total figure at over 800,000 women employed in such operational roles. Bute Mendeluva taught tank driving at the main tank school at Tankograd in 1942, while in the nearby tank factories women worked twelve-hour shifts. In the field, Ekatania Petlyuk was the first woman to drive a tank in the Red Army, while Mariya Oktyabr'skaya bought a tank from her personal savings and fought as its commander in the rank of Guards Sergeant, until she was mortally wounded near Krynka in January 1944 (she was posthumously made a Heroine of the Soviet Union). At the age of twenty-five, First Lieutenant Ekaterina Zelenko had become the deputy commander of a squadron in No. 135 Bomber Wing and notched up over forty sorties in the first few weeks after the German invasion of Russia. First Lieutenant Lidiya Litvyak commanded a flight of fighter aircraft, completed 268 sorties and destroyed eleven enemy aircraft before she herself was shot down. Katyuska Mikailova was a medical training instructor with the Soviet marines and she accompanied them during the storming of the Ilok fortress on the Danube, using a machine gun to great effect.

Another remarkable Russian female soldier was Mila Pavilchenko, who was known to the Germans as the 'Bolshevik Valkyrie'. A young history student, she came into prominence during the siege of Odessa, where she killed 180 German soldiers with her sniper's rifle. Her exploits were quickly seized upon for propaganda and she was the subject of a documentary film, which spread her fame throughout the USSR and into British and American newspapers. She continued to kill 'Hitlerists', one duel with an expert German sniper at Sevastopol lasting for just over two days – she killed him in the end, then crawled to his position and found a notebook on his body which showed that he had accounted for over 500 British, French and Red Army soldiers. Early in 1942, she was requested to report to Moscow to meet Joseph Stalin and also to be part of a delegation of Soviet soldiers who had been invited by Eleanor Roosevelt to visit the United States. She was a great hit in America, telling one audience that she was twenty-five years old and had killed 309 Nazis and that she hoped the US would start the Second Front soon and not '... hide behind my back for too long!'

Israeli women soldiers have fought alongside their menfolk through all the vicissitudes of that nation but although they are also allowed to be part of a tank crew, there are still restrictions as to where they are sent – for fear of them possibly becoming prisoners. In early 1996, the British army revealed that it had begun to study the Israeli use of all-female tank crews, as part of a wide-ranging analysis to determine whether women should fight with armour, artillery and infantry regiments.

In Germany Chancellor Kohl's coalition allies, the Free Democrats, have been campaigning for sex equality in the armed forces, demanding that women should be allowed to serve on the same terms as men. However, so far, the very conventional Germans have dismissed the idea of women combatants out of hand; they remain in the medical units and bands and are not allowed to carry weapons, even for self defence. Other politicians have accused the Free Democrats of 'posturing' in taking up sex equality in the army and Volker Beck (spokesman for the Greens), according to one newspaper, says that the Free Democrats 'should be worrying why they have the smallest proportion of woman MPs of any party, instead of brooding whether Lily Marlene, instead of standing underneath the lantern, by the barrack gate, should stand guard directly in front of the gate with a gun in her hand'.

During the Vietnam war, Duong Thu Huong, a twenty-one-year-old girl led the Communist Youth Brigade in the most heavily bombarded front, living underground in tunnels alongside the North Vietnamese troops.

Although no other individual names have so far come to light, no doubt there were many other women fighting for their country alongside the regular troops.

The only armies who have totally done away with discrimination between the genders are Belgium, Canada, Holland and Norway – and in these armies *any* soldier can be sent to a combat area.

A glance at any parade photograph of practically any modern army is likely to show more than a sprinkling of female faces among the ranks. Moreover, some guerrilla armies deliberately set out to recruit combat units that are entirely female.

Discounting the obvious problems that inevitably will occur when men and women share the same stressful tasks, in close proximity and amid the blood, muck and mire of the battlefield, where the niceties of such considerations as separate toilet facilities are impossible, the main stumbling block is the basic act of killing or being killed. How will the morale of a unit be affected by the death of women soldiers? How will female soldiers feel about killing others? Is killing really any different for a woman as opposed to a man? History has shown that, stripped of all prejudice, the differences, if there are any, are illogical and do not hold up to close examination.

CHAPTER 13

Fact or Fiction?

Although the majority of the stories related here can be verified by factual evidence, there are a few that must raise doubts even in the most charitable mind, and must be classified as unsubstantiated. The following three examples, therefore, involve a measure of conjecture, even though the heroines concerned have by now become legends in their own countries.

The first, and oldest, story comes from Scotland, and appears to have been started deliberately by the English in order to discredit Bonnie Prince Charlie. The tale of Jenny Cameron was seized upon by both sides, one making her out to be an ogress, the other a heroine. At best, therefore, she may be described as a figment of popular imagination.

The second is quite different. The story of Lucy Brewer allegedly stems from her own pen, and it is those in authority who now seek to discredit her. They point to obvious weaknesses in her account, but there seems to be enough positive evidence to give her the benefit of the doubt.

The final story, of 'Colonel' Barker, is of a proven modern-day hoaxer, who was definitely a rogue to boot. Her actions were so flagrantly dishonest that they should not be allowed to tarnish the reputation of the many brave women who did indeed fight in battle and are remembered in this book.

Jenny Cameron

On 19 August 1745, the young Prince Charles waited impatiently in his highland refuge in Glenfinnan. All day he had expected the arrival of the first of the clansmen whom he had ordered to rally to his standard. At approximately 4 o'clock he heard the skirl of the pipes and watched, with feelings of relief and anticipation, as the kilted highlanders of the Camerons and MacDonalds, some 12,000 of them in all, marched proudly into the glen with their banners waving.

A popular story of the time said that at the head of 250 Cameron clay-mores rode a splendidly equipped warrior:

'She rode into camp on a bay gelding decked out in green trappings, trimmed with gold. She wore a sea-green riding habit with scarlet lappets edged with gold. Her hair was tied behind in loose buckles, and covered by a velvet cap with scarlet feathers. In her hand, in lieu of a whip, she carried a sword.'

The prince ran forward to greet her personally and she replied to his courtesy with a smart military salute. The woman was named as the 'brave Miss Jenny Cameron' who was about to lead her clansmen in action at the battles of Prestonpans, Falkirk and Culloden.

Unfortunately, the story was not entirely true; nor was another tale, also put about by Whig propagandists, that she was the prince's mistress. Jean (Jenny) Cameron was the only daughter of Alan Cameron, of Glendessary, born about 1714 in her parents' house at Acharn in Morvern. She was 'a genteel, well looked, handsome woman, with a pair of pretty eyes, and hair as black as jet'. But although she was certainly present at Glenfinnan at the raising of the standard, she never accompanied the army, nor followed the camp, nor was she ever with the prince except in public when he held court in Edinburgh.

The stories were all fabricated by 'Grub Street's scandalmongers' to damage the prince's reputation. How effective they were is uncertain, though they were widely circulated. But one interesting version of the tale was sent to us by Mr Iain Thornber of Ardtornish, Morvern, who has done a considerable amount of research into Jenny Cameron's life.

By strange coincidence, when Prince Charles was besieging Stirling Castle, there was a Miss or Mrs Jenny Cameron who carried on a milliner's business in Edinburgh. Hearing that one of her relatives in the Highland army was lying wounded in the Jacobite camp, she set out for Stirling with the intention of paying him a visit. The day following her arrival in camp, the Duke of Cumberland took command of the English army in Edinburgh, and moved northwards, leaving the milliner to be captured by one of the English outposts on her return to the city boundaries. On being arrested and disclosing her name, the officer commanding immediately jumped to the conclusion that he had secured as a prize a celebrated Highland heroine. Cumberland quickly heard of the capture and writing from Stirling on 2 February 1746, to the Duke of Newcastle, he stated, '… we have taken about twenty of their sick here, and the famous Miss Jenny Cameron, whom I propose to send to Edinburgh for the Lord Clerk to examine as I fancy she may be a useful evidence against them, if a little threatened". From this letter of Cumberland's it is clear that the English army was completely taken in by its own propaganda.

Cumberland was as good as his word and Jenny found herself in Edinburgh Castle where she remained until 15 November 1746, when she was released on bail. If her living conditions were sub-standard at least she was in good company, for according to *Prisoners of the '45* (Scottish History Society, 1928, Vol. 1, p. 69), she shared her quarters with such distinguished prisoners as Lady Strathallan, the Duchess of Perth, Lady Ogilvy, the Earl of Kellie and other notable Jacobites. On being released she returned to her long neglected shop, and business poured in: 'all the city crowding to buy ribbons, gloves, fans, etc' on the mistaken notion that she had been Prince Charlie's mistress, a fiction she did not attempt to contradict. She appears to have remained in the public eye, for *The Scots Magazine* noted her death in Ghent in 1767 and even ran an obituary notice, which read 'At Ghent, Miss Jenny Cameron, famous for her attachment to the young Pretender.'

According to Mr Thornber, there were others who posed as the famous Jenny Cameron, particularly one in 1786, who wore men's clothes, having a wooden leg, and subsequently dying in a 'stair fir' somewhere in Canongate Edinburgh.

So that appears to be the true story of Jenny Cameron. Yet her martial prowess still lives on in Scottish mythology, as in a Highland song composed in her honour which tells how:

> *'Miss Jenny Cameron*
> *She put her belt and hangar on*
> *And away to the Young Pretender.'*

Lucy Brewer, leatherneck or liar?

In the summer of 1815 a series of small pamphlets appeared in various towns in New England, the first series being entitled: 'An Affecting Narrative – Louisa Baker'. It was followed by another series called 'The Adventures of Lucy Brewer' in which the author explained that Louisa Baker was her nom de plume and that her given name was Lucy Brewer. The two pamphlets were put together under the title 'The Female Marine' and have from time to time reappeared under various other, slightly different, names, but the subject matter has always been the same, namely about a girl who masqueraded as an American marine in the War of 1812.

Lucy Brewer was born in Plymouth County, Massachusetts, in 1793. A simple farm girl, she was a vivacious youngster and at the tender age of sixteen fell under the spell of a young local rake, who seduced her. Her family warned her about him but Lucy was convinced that she could take care of herself and that anyway her sweetheart would marry her. Unfortunately she was wrong and he deserted her once she became pregnant. To escape from her strict Puritan family, and the disgrace she had brought upon them, she ran away to Boston, hoping to find some work. She had a rough time for a while but eventually she was taken in by a kindly middle-aged woman who lived in a large house with lots of 'daughters', all of whom appeared to be the same age. Poor naive Lucy did not discover that she was in a brothel until it was too late. Her baby died at birth and when she tried to leave she was pointedly told that she would have to work in order to pay for all the kindness and hospitality that she had received. And 'work' she did, although her customers were the finest gentlemen in Boston!

It took Lucy three years before she was able to find a means of escape. The War of 1812 had just begun and one of her clients – a young marine officer – fell in love with her and expressed a desire to help her to get away. Over a drink one evening, as they chatted about the adventures of Deborah Sampson who, as already mentioned, had served as a soldier in the War of Independence, Lucy's lover offered to procure her some sailor's clothing so that she could 'escape to sea'. Resorting to all the normal methods of disguising the female form, namely cutting short her hair, binding her breasts and wearing a waistcoat and tight underdrawers, she left the brothel and found herself able to pass as a man without any difficulty. In a waterfront tavern she met a naval recruiting party and was quickly signed on under the name of George Baker. She says that she succeeded by 'an artful stratagem' to avoid the 'search' (medical inspection) to which new recruits were now subjected, and was issued with her marine uniform and advance of pay. She was posted to a marine company commanded by a Lieutenant William S. Bush, for whom she clearly must have developed a crush, describing him as 'one of the most humane and experienced officers in the American navy'. Sadly, her idol was killed in action not long afterwards. She trained as a marksman, which meant that her normal battle station was in the ship's rigging, over ninety feet above the swaying, rolling deck. It was quite a daunting prospect for a young girl, but she soon became expert: 'In the use of my arms I made great proficiency and soon learned to load and discharge my musket with an expertness not surpassed by any in the corps.'

Her company was posted to serve on board the USS *Constitution*, a forty-four gun, 1450-ton frigate, under the command of Captain Isaac Hull. It was already one of the most famous ships in the American navy and Captain Hull took every opportunity to enhance his reputation as a brave and resourceful commander. Putting to sea in mid-July, the *Constitution* was soon involved in a spectacular sea chase in which they managed to outwit and outsail a British squadron. 'I suffered a little confinement from seasickness so peculiar to fresh hands,' records Lucy on this exhilarating first voyage, 'which was all the illness I experienced during the whole cruise.'

On their return Hull did not stay in port for long, and they slipped out again early in August. This time they were involved in a fierce battle with HMS *Guerrière*, a British frigate of very similar size and firepower. It was Lucy's first engagement and she wrote:

'I was at this time busily employed in the topmast, playing my faithful musket with the best success whenever the smoke would permit me to see a bluejacket of the enemy. In the heat of the action a grapeshot struck and splintered the butt of my musket. It was noticed by one of my comrades who stood within a few feet of me. He exclaimed "Never mind George. You

170

have won laurels sufficient to recommend you to the pretty
girls when you return to port!"'

In her description of the engagement Lucy shows a remarkable grasp of the
language of the sea, talking learnedly about 'a ship under easy sail, close
hauled to the wind ... all her guns, which were double shotted with round
and grape....' Critics have claimed that she copied the entire description of
the battle from Captain Hull's official report. But how could she have had
access to this?

Surprising as it may seem, Lucy, like her English counterpart
Hannah Snell, succeeded in concealing her true identity from the rest of
the ship's crew. She was perhaps assisted in this by the fact that in those
days the company of marines normally had quarters separate from the
rest of the crew. The marines also kept aloof from the ordinary seamen
and occupied bunks rather than hammocks, sleeping in cabins or 'state-
rooms' with six marines to a room. Moreover, they ate at their own exclusive mess tables.

When she went ashore after the battle, it was evident that the
members of her own sex could not see through her disguise. She even met
girls from the brothel where she had worked, without any hint of recognition. 'In more than one instance I was actually in the company of girls who
were lately my associates, but who did not identify my person – so artfully
did I disguise myself.'

Most sailors in those days let their hair grow long as there were no
barbers on board and wore their tresses in a pigtail to keep them out of the
way in the wind and spray, so Lucy was able to let her hair grow normally.
Indeed, she found the marine disguise so convenient that she wrote: 'I felt
no disposition to resume my former dress or to return to that wicked course
of life which I now more than ever detested.'

It was during the next cruise of the *Constitution* that Lucy's secret was
almost discovered. In the battle with the British frigate, HMS *Java*, off the
coast of Brazil in December 1812, she was once again stationed in the 'tops'
and fired her musket no less than nineteen times, '... which as I now had
learned to take pretty exact aim, must I think have done some execution'. As
she was descending, after four hours of battle, the exhausted girl tripped in
the shrouds, missed her footing and fell overboard:

171

'Not knowing how to swim, I sank immediately, a boat was sent to my relief, but before they could recover me and get me on board, life was almost extinct. As soon as they had succeeded in getting me on the deck, as I had not the strength to do it myself, some of my shipmates were ordered to strip off my clothes and to furnish me with a dry suit. And they had nearly divested me of my outer dress when I mustered sufficient strength to beg them to desist, as I then felt able to effect it myself.'

Lucy went on serving on the *Constitution* for the next three years until the end of the war, and took part in the ship's final battle off the west coast of Africa in February 1815. Having received her wages and prize money which amounted to nearly a thousand dollars, she decided to rehabilitate herself as a female. She also found that she was homesick and, after six years' absence, went home to be happily reunited with her parents, who apparently forgave all her previous indiscretions.

It was at this time that she wrote her first book, but even this new career failed to satisfy her adventurous spirit. Deciding that it was still far easier to travel as a man, she disguised herself once again and took the stage-coach to New York. En route, a young midshipmen, the worse for drink, began to be offensive towards a young female passenger named Anne West. He also challenged an elderly passenger, who tried to remonstrate with him, to a duel. That was too much for Lucy to endure. She informed the drunken officer that if he did not apologise to the young lady she would take him on herself, with pistols, at twenty paces! The owner of the inn at which they were spending the night wanted no bloodshed on his premises, so Lucy managed to extract an apology from the officer, much to the delight of her fellow passengers. She met Anne again during her stay in New York and, still in disguise, was taken home to meet the family. Her parents and brother Robert were clearly impressed by the 'gallant young gentleman' who had saved Anne's honour.

Lucy returned home and decided once and for all to stop dressing as a man and to become a woman again. But fate had not finished with her. Contemporary critics of her book argued that no woman could possibly live on board a ship for three years without being discovered, and that in any event no one called 'Louise Baker' had ever existed.

In order to prove them wrong, Lucy published a new edition of her little book, this time under her own name, adding not only her latest adventure on the stage-coach journey, but also her real name and address. Soon after these new revelations had been published, she had a surprise visitor in the shape of Robert West, who immediately proposed marriage. Lucy accepted, they were wed in 1816 and, as in all good stories, 'they lived happily ever after'.

When we wrote to the US Marine Corps for help with background material for Lucy's story, they were careful to point out that as far as they were concerned, she was just a myth. In 1947, the authenticity of the Lucy Brewer story had been challenged and two historians of the US Marine Corps assigned to make exhaustive research of the subject. What had sparked off this investigation was the naming of one of the main streets in the marine camp – Camp Lejeune – 'Lucy Brewer Avenue'. As one of the two historians, John L. Zimmerman explains: 'I think it would have been wise if someone had looked into the matter of Lucy before nailing up the street markers.' He goes on to examine her story objectively, stressing the expertise with which this young lady appears so quickly to have picked up the language of the sea. But he questions the remark made by Lucy's compatriot in the 'tops' when her musket stock was hit by fire, saying: ' Now by the shin bones of O'Bannon if any marine in the navy, in any battle in history said that, or anything like it, to a fellow marine, then I will pin a red rose to my stacking swivel and go sit in Pershing Square in the soft summer evening.'

On the other hand, other well-known military historians, such as John Laffin, have rushed to Lucy's defence; it is clear from his book *Women in Battle* that he firmly believes she did exist. As with the rest of this book we have deliberately not passed judgement on Lucy. But if Her Majesty's 'Jollies' had their bold Hannah, then is it so inconceivable that the President's 'Leathernecks' should not have had their Lucy?

Colonel Sir Victor Barker, DSO

'Colonel' Barker was born on the island of Jersey, the daughter of a well-respected local resident, and in 1918 married an Australian army officer. The marriage broke up and Mrs Arkell-Smith, as she was then called, went to live in Warminster, Wiltshire. There she met and fell in love with a Mr Crouch. Although they were never married, she lived with him as his common law wife and they had two children. But this relationship did not last. In 1922 she left Crouch and, having adopted male clothing, went to live in Littlehampton. She now called herself 'Sir Victor Barker' and on 14 November 1923 went through a marriage ceremony with the daughter of a local chemist. The two women lived together as man and wife for about four years and then Lady Barker left her 'husband' and returned home to her father. Although she later swore that she had never realised that her 'husband' was in fact another woman, there is evidence to suggest that she did know the truth, so presumably it was a lesbian relationship.

'Sir Victor' also passed herself off as an army captain and later promoted herself to the rank of colonel, 'earning' a number of medals on the way. These included the Distinguished Service Order – Britain's third highest award for bravery. In 1927, she became associated with the National Fascist Movement and was summoned for an offence against the Firearms Act. It is said that she appeared in court with her eyes bandaged and being led by a companion. She explains that she was suffering from temporary blindness as the result of old war wounds and the strain of having to go to court had brought on the trouble again. Apparently she won the sympathy of the court because she was acquitted. No one in court that day seems to have been aware that not only was Colonel Barker not a wounded hero but not even a man!

Shortly after this appearance at the Old Bailey she was charged with bankruptcy and her strange secret was revealed. Although it could be said that she had distinctly feminine features, her photographs all show that she certainly filled out the crisp, white, stiff-fronted shirt of her immaculate mess kit in a very masculine manner!

CHAPTER 14

Women Warriors in Song and Verse

T he seventeenth and eighteenth centuries produced a marvellous crop of ballads, folk songs and poems about the exploits of contemporary women warriors. Most of the examples from the small selection reproduced here were published in the *Roxburghe Ballads*, edited by J. Woodfall Ebsworth and published by the Ballad Society in 1893. Others, such as the poem 'The Female Soldier', which tells the story of Hannah Snell, come from contemporary magazines.

Female smugglers and robbers were also the subjects of similar ballads, one aptly being named 'Dick Turpin's sister'.

1. The Gallant She-Soldiers or
A brief Relation of a faithful-hearted Woman

Who for the Love that she bore to her Husband, attired her selfe in Man's Apparell and so became a Souldier, and marcht along with him through Ireland, France and Spain, and never was known to be a Woman till at the last she being quartered neere unto Tower-hill, in London, where she brought forth a gallant Man-Child, to the wonder of all her fellow Souldiers. Of her valiant actions, honest carriage, and excellent behaviour; You shall presently heare (if you please).

You noble-minded Souldiers all, that faithful are and true,
   This Ditty I have written for Love I beare to you;
Concerning of a Woman that was upright and just,
   Honest in her actions, and true unto her trust.
Seek England, Scotland and all the world about,
   There's hardly such another to be found out.

Her husband was a Souldier, and to the wars did goe,
    And she would be his Comrade, the truth of all is so.
She put on Man's apparel, and bore him company,
    As many in the Army for truth can testify.
Seek England, Scotland and all the worlds about,
    There's hardly such another to be found out.

With Musket on her Shoulder, her part she acted then,
    And every one supposed that she had been a Man;
Her Bandaleers about her neck, and sword hang'd by her side:
    In many brave adventures her valour had been try'd.

But now behold with wonder what hap'ned at the last,
    After much time in merriment she had in London past,
She found by several passages her selfe to be with child;
    T'was by her honest Husband, she could not be beguil'd.

Yet secretly she kept it, so long as ever she could,
    Till such a time a Commander her be teeming did behold;
'What is the reason Tom' quoth he 'that you are grown so fatt?'
    'T'is strong Beere and Tobacco, Sir, which is the cause of that.'

But when her painefull houre had come, that she must
      delivered be,
    The Women flockt about her, her grievances to see;
Her breeches then were pulled off, and there began the wonder'
    For in a short time after she was fallen quite in sunder.

The sixteenth day of July, as true reports do say,
    The Souldier was delivered of a lusty chopping boy;
The people that heares this newes, each day do flock and run,
    To see the Woman-souldier and her little pretty Son.

Some gives her beds and blankets, her Baby for to Nurse,
    Some gives her wholesome dyet, and money in her purse,
All them that comes to see her, their bounty doth bestow;
    Indeed it is but fitting that they should all doe so.

To draw to a conclusion, I wish in heart and mind
    That Women to their Husbands were every one so kind,
As she was to her Sweet-heart, her love to him was so,
    That she forsooke all others, along with him to goe.

Whereby we may perceive and see, and very well approve,
    There's nothing in ye world can be compar'd to faithful Love;
The Hammer will breake Marble, and Hunger breake stone-wall,
    But Love is sole Commander, and Conqueror of all.

This ballad (here shortened by several verses) was written in 1655 reputedly by Lawrence Price and below it was the following note:

All that are desirous to see the young Souldier and his Mother, let them repair to the sign of the Black-Smith's-Arms, in East Smithfield, neere unto Tower-hill, in London, and enquire for Mr Clarke, for that was the Woman's name.
                              (London, Printed for Richard Burton, in Smithfield)

2. The famous Woman Drummer;
– or The Valiant proceedings of a Maid which was deep in Love with a Souldier, and how she went with him to the wars; and also many brave actions that she performed, after he had made her his wife; that here be exprest in this ensuing ditty.

Of a Maiden that was deep in love with a Souldier brave and bold sir,
    I'll tell you here as true a tale, as ever hath been told, Sir;
And what brave actions she perform'd, after she was his Wife, Sir;
    And how she did behave her selfe, to save her Husband's life Sir.
She marcht with him, in wet and dry, in Winter and in Summer,
    For he was then a Musketier, and she became a Drummer.

When first this couple fell in love, a bargain she did make, sir,
    That when that he had need of her, she would not him forsake, sir;
And so they went for two Comrades, most lovingly together,
    And plaid their parts most actively, like two birds of one feather.
She marcht with him, in wet and dry, in Winter and in Summer,
    For he was then a Musketier, and she became a Drummer.

They have been both in Ireland, in Spain, and famous France, sir,
    Where lustily she beat her Drum, her honour to advance, sir;
Whilst cannons roar'd, and bullets flye, as thick as hail from sky, sir,
    She never fear'd her forraign Foes, when her Comrade was nigh, sir.
She stood the brunts in heat and cold, in winter and in summer,
    Her Husband was a Musketier, and she was then a Drummer.

In every place that she did come, she shew'd herselfe so valiant,
    And few men might compare with her, her actions were so gallant;
She manage could her sword full well, and to advance a pike, sir,
    But for the beating of a Drum, you seldome saw the like sir.
In frost and snow, in wet or dry, in winter and in summer,
    Her husband was a Musketier, and she a famous Drummer.

For Love is such a powerful thing, if it be rightly given,
    There cannot be a better gift under the copes of Heaven,
So now, brave Souldiers all, adieu! remember what is spoken,
    Come buy my songs, and send them to your Sweet-heartys for a token.
Her Husband was a Musketier, and she a warlike Drummer,
    I would that I had such a mate, to walk with me this Summer.

(shortened by several verses) c.1679

3. The Maiden Warrier
*or The Damsel's Resolution to fight in field by the side of Jockey
her entire Love.*

Valiant Jockey's march'd away,
    To fight the foe with great Mackay;
Leaving me, poor soul, alas! forlorn,
    To curse the hour I e're was born;
But I swear I'se follow too,
    And dearest Jockey's fate pursue,
Near him be to guard his precious life,
    Never Scot had sike a wife;

Sword I'se wear, I'se cut my hair,
   Tann my cheeks that once were thought so fair,
In Soldier's weed to him I speed,
   Never sike a Trooper crost the Tweed.

Trumpet sound to victory,
   I'se kill myself the next Dundee;
Love and rage, and fate do's all agree,
   To do some glorious thing by me;
Great Bellona take my part,
   Fame and glory steel my heart,
That for our bonny Scotland's geud,
   Some brave action may deserve my bloud;
Nought shall appear of female fear,
   Fighting by his side I love so dear;
All the world shall own, that ne'er was known
   Sike a pretty Lass! this thousand year.

                        (Tom D'Urfey 1689)

4. Pretty Polly Oliver's Ramble

One night as Polly Oliver lay musing in bed,
   A comical fancy came into her head,
'Neither father nor mother shall make me false prove,
   I'll list for a Soldier, and follow my love.'

Early next morning this fair maid arose,
   She dressed herself in a man's suit of clothes,
Coat, waistcoat, and breeches, and sword by her side,
   On her father's black gelding like a dragoon she did ride.

She rid till she came to fair London town,
   She dismounted her horse at the sign of the crown,
The first that came down was a man from above
   The next that came down was Polly Oliver's love.

'Good evening, good evening, kind Captain' said she;
　　'Here's a letter from your true love, Polly Oliver', said she.
He opened the letter, and a guinea there was found,
　　'For you and your companions, to drink her health round.'

Supper being ended, she held down her head,
　　And called for a candle to light her to bed;
The Captain made this reply, 'I have a bed at my ease,
　　You may lie with me, countryman, if you please.'

'To lie with a Captain is a dangerous thing,
　　I am a new enlisted Soldier to fight for our King;
To fight for our King by sea and by land;
　　Since you are my Captain, I'll be at your command.'

Early next morning this fair maid arose,
　　And drest herself in her own suit of clothes;
And down stairs she came, from the chamber above,
　　Saying, 'Here is Polly Oliver, your own true love.'

He at first was surprised, then laughed at the fun,
　　And then they were married and things were all done;
'If I lay with you the first night, the fault it was mine;
　　I hope to please you better, love, for now it is my time.'

5. Billy Taylor

　　Four and twenty brisk young fellows
　　　　Drest they were in rich array,
　　And they took poor Billy Taylor,
　　　　Whom they press'd and sent to sea.

　　And his truelove follow'd after
　　　　Under the name of Richard Car,
　　Her lily-white hands were bedaub'd all over
　　　　With the nasty pitch and tar.

180

Now behold the first engagement
    Bold she fought among the rest
Till the wind did blow her jacket,
    And discovered her lily-white breast.

When the captain came to view it
    Says he 'What wind has blown you here?'
'Sir, I be come to seek my truelove
    Whom you press'd I love so dear.'

'If you be come to seek your treasure
    Tell to me his name, I pray.'
'Sir, his name is Billy Taylor
    Whom you press'd and sent to sea.'

'If his name is Billy Taylor,
    He is both cruel and severe,
For rise up early in the morning
    And you'll see him with his lady fair.'

With that she rose up early next morning,
    Early by the break of day,
And there she saw bold Billy Taylor
    Dancing with his lady gay.

With that she called for sword and pistol,
    Which did come at her command,
And there she shot bold Billy Taylor
    With his truelove in his hand.

When the captain came for to know it
    He very much applauded her for what she had done
And immediately made her the first lieutenant
    Of the glorious Thunder Bumb.

6. The Press Gang

It's of a rich gentleman in London did dwell
　　He had but one daughter, a most beautiful gel
Three squires came acourting and she refused all
　　'I will marry a sailor, that's proper and tall.

'Now father, dear father, now hinder me not
　　I'll marry a sailor, I hope will be my lot.
To see him in his charm with a smile on his face
　　I am sure that sailor he is no disgrace.'

They walk-ed out and they talk-ed both night and day
　　They walk-ed and talk-ed and fixed the wedding day,
The old man overheard it and these words he did say
　　'He shan't marry my daughter, I'll press him to sea.'

As they were a-walking towards the church door
　　The press gang overtook him and from her side tore.
They pressed this young fellow all on the salt sea
　　Instead of getting married he sorrowed for she.

She cut off her hair and she altered her clothes
　　And to the press-master she immediately goes,
Saying 'Press-master, press-master do you want a man?
　　I am willing and ready to do all I can.'

Then she ship-ped on board the very same ship
　　Her true love for a mess mate so quickly she take,
True love for for a mess-mate you quickly shall hear;
　　She sleep by his side for a full half year.

Now one morning, one morning as these two arose
　　They got into discourse as they put on their clothes.
'Once I had a sweetheart, in London lived she,
　　But it's her cruel father that pressed me to sea.'

She looked into his face and looked him quite start
'Say now, I believe you are my sweetheart.
For now we'll get married before our ship's crew
We won't care for father or all he can do.'

(The Press Gang is a reduced version of a ballad of fifteen verses called 'The Sailor's Misfortune and Happy Marriage'.)

7. Canada I.O.

It's of a gallant lady gay all in her tender years,
　　She was courted by a sailor bold, 'tis true she loved him dear,
But how to get to sea with him, the way she did not know,
　　She fain would see that pretty place called Canada I.O.

She bargained with some sailors bold all for a purse of gold,
　　Then they conveyed this lady gay all down into the hold,
We'll dress her up in sailor's clothes if she to sea will go;
　　She soon shall see that pretty place called Canada I.O.

But when her true love heard the news an angry man was he,
　　He did curse and swear to the sailors in that good ship's company;
'I'll tie you hand and foot, my love, and overboard you'll go;
　　You ne'er shall see that pretty place called Canada I.O.

Then up and spoke our captain bold, 'Oh that can never be,
　　For if you drown this lady gay then hang-ed you shall be.
We'll dress her up in sailor's clothes if she to sea will go
　　And she will see that pretty place called Canada I.O.'

She had not been in Canada for scarcely half a year,
　　Before our captain married her and took her for his dear,
She dresses up in silks and lace and makes a noble show,
　　She's the grandest captain's lady now in Canada I.O.

8. The Female Soldier

Hannah in breeks behaved so well
    That none her softer sex could tell;
Nor was her policy confounded,
    When hear the mark of nature wounded;
Which proves, what men will scarce admit
    That women are for secrets fit.

That healthy blood could keep so long,
    Amidst young fellows hale and strong
Demonstrates, tho' a seeming wonder,
    That love to courage truckles under.

O how her bed mate bit his lips,
    And mark'd the spreading of her hips;
And curs'd the blindness of his youth,
    When she confess'd the naked truth.

Her Fortitude, to no man's second,
    To woman's honour must be reckon'd.
Twelve wounds! 'twas half great Caesar's number,
    That made his corpse the ground encumber.
How many men, for heroes nurst,
    Had left their colours at the first?

'Twas thought Achilles' greatest glory,
    That Homer rose to sing his story,
And Alexander mourn'd his lot,
    That no such bard could then be got.
But Hannah's praise no Homer needs;
    She lives to sing her proper Deeds.

(This poem appeared in *The Gentlemen's Magazine* 1750, and was kindly supplied by the Librarian of the Royal United Services Institute)

184

Hannah herself sang songs during her stage performance and one of the verses went as follows:

> In the midst of blood and slaughter,
>> Bravely fighting for my King,
> Facing death from every quarter
>> Fame and conquest home to bring.
> Sure, you'll own 'tis more than common,
>> And the world proclaims it, too,
> Never yet did any woman
>> More for love and glory do.

Acknowledgements

We would like to thank the following for their invaluable help in the preparation of this book: The Belgian Embassy, London; The Bradford Metropolitan Library; The British Library; The British Museum; The City of Manchester Public Library; The Chilean Embassy, London; The Frans Hals Museum, Haarlem; R. H. Bennett Studio, Wisconsin; HQ United States Marine Corps; The Irish Embassy, London; The Imperial War Museum; Musée National de la Légion d'Honneur, Paris; Home HQ 15th/19th The King's Royal Hussars; The National Army Museum; The National Maritime Museum; The New York Public Library; Photographie Bulloz, Paris; The RAMC Historical Museum; The Royal Marines Museum; RHQ The Royal Hampshire Regiment; RHQ The Queen's Lancashire Regiment; The Scottish United Services Museum; Service Historique de l'Armée de Terre; US Army Military History Institute; US Library of Congress; US National Archives and Record Service; US Field Artillery Journal; US Army Field Artillery Museum, Fort Sill; The West Point Museum; and our son Adam Forty for all his help to his computer-illiterate mother.

Index

A

Agustina, 28, 32–37
Amazon(s), 9
American Civil War, 46 et seq, 63 et
 seq
American Revolutionary War, see
 War of Independence
American servicewomen, 161 et
 seq
Andate, 10
Angelsey (Mona), 12
Angers, 43, 44
Arc, Joan of, see Joan of Arc
Arundel, Lady Blanche, 25
Aston Exchange Herald newspaper,
 103

B

Bankes, Lady Mary, 19–23
Barker, Colonel Sir Victor,
 173–174
Barreau, Alexandrine, 120–121
Barry, Major-General James,
 134–139
Bedford, Duke of, 30 et seq
Belsen, 158
Bonnie Prince Charlie, 167
Bonny, Anne, 94–95

Bordereau, Renée, 42–46
Botchkareva, Marie Yashka,
 128–133, 163
Boudicca, 10–16
Bouvreuil Castle, 32
Bowen, Captain Essex, 87, 88
Boyd, Belle, 49–55
Brewer, Lucy, 166, 169–173
British servicewomen, 159 et seq
Brownell, Kadie, 47
Burke, Sir Richard, 17 et seq
Byron, Lord, 37

C

Cameron, Jenny, 166–168
Canada, 138
Cashier, Albert, see Jenny Hidgers
Cavell, Edith Louisa, 152
Cerneau, Yvonne Claire,
 157–158
Charles I, King, 19, 23
Clarke, Amy, 47
Clayton, Frances L., 47
Corfu, 137
Colchester, 12
Corbin, Margaret 'Molly', 74–75
Corfe Castle, 19 et seq, 22, 23
Cromwell, Oliver, 19 et seq, 146

D

Dalbiac, Susanna, 68–71

Davies, Christina, 57–61

d'Eon, Chevalier, 147–150

Delilah, 146

Dumouriez, General, 112 et seq

Detzliffin, Anne Sophia, 106–108

Devens, 'Michigan' Bridget, 46

Doyle, Fanny, 74, 75–76

E

Earies, Sir William, 20, 21

Edinburgh University, 134 et seq

Elizabeth I, Queen, 18, 146

Elizabeth, Empress of Russia, 148

English Civil War, 19 et seq, 24 et seq

Ensign Nun, see Catalina de Erauso

Erauso, Catalina de, 101–103

Etheridge, Annie, 48–49

F

Fernig, Félicité and Théophile de, 111-114

Figueur, Thérèse, 114–116

Fourcade, Marie-Madeleine, 152, 153

Front Royal, 51 et seq

G

Gannett, Deborah Sampson, 108-111

Garibaldi, Anita, 78–84

Garibaldi, Guiseppe, 78, 79 et seq

German servicewomen, 164

Granville, Christine, 153–156

H

Haarlem, 25 et seq

Hasselaar Kenau, 25–27

Hari, Mata, 151, 152

Hessel, Phoebe, 118–120

Hidgers, Jenny, 47

I

Iceni, 10 et seq

Independence, War of, 108 et seq, 150

Israeli servicewomen, 164

J

Jackson, General 'Stonewall', 51–53, 64

Jacqueline, see Yvonne Cerneau

Joan of Arc, 28–32, 133

K

Kincaid, 71 et seq

Knowsley, 24

Kowerski, Andrew, 154 et seq, 156

L

La Pucelle, see Joan of Arc

Lathom House, 24

Lawrence, Dorothy, 134, 139–145

Litvyak, Lidiya, 163

Livermore, Mary A., 46

London, 13

Louis XV, King, 148,149

Ludwig, Mary, see Molly Pitcher

M

Maquis, 42

Michel, Louise, 28, 37–41

Mikailova, Katyuska, 163

N

Napoleon, 62

Nightingale, Florence, 137

O

Oktyabr'skaya, Mariya, 163

Oliver, 'Pretty Polly', 56, 180

O'Malley, Grace, 16–18

Orleans, 29 et seq

P

Palafox y Melzi, Don José, 32, 35

Paris, 141, 142

Paris Commune, 28, 37 et seq

Paulinus, Caius Suetonius, see
    Roman Governor of Britain

Pavilchenko, Mila, 163

Petluk, Ekatania, 163

Pirates, 91 et seq

Pitcher, Molly, 74, 75–78

Prasutagus, 10, 11

R

Read, Mary, 91–94

Red Virgin, see Louise Michel

Rheims, 30

Romans, 10 et seq

Roman Governor of Britain, 12 et
    seq, 15

Ross, Mother, see Christina
    Davies

Roundheads, 20 et seq, 24, 25

Royal Engineers, 139, 143 et seq

Royal Marines, 95 et seq

Royal Hospital, Chelsea, 61, 100

Russian Revolution, 132

S

St Albans, 13

Sandes, Flora, 122–128

Sanson, Odette, 158

Saragossa, 28, 32–37

Schellenck, Mary, 61–63

Serbian Army, 122 et seq

Smith, Lady Juana, 68, 71–74

Smith, Lieutenant-General Sir
    Harry, 72 et seq

Snell, Hannah, 95–100, 175, 184,
    185

SOE (Special Operations Executive),
    42, 155, 158

Song and verse, 175–185

South Africa, 74, 135 et seq

Soviet servicewomen, 163

Spies, 146–158

Stanley, Charlotte, Countess of
    Derby, 23–24

Szabo, Violette, 158

T

Tacitus, 12 et seq, 14, 15

Talbot, Mary Anne, 86–91

Taylor, Sarah, 103–106

Toledo, Don Frederick of, 26 et seq

U

US Marine Corps, 170–173

V

Velázquez, Loreta, 63–68
La Vendée, 42 et seq
Verse and song 175–185

W

Wake, Nancy, 42
War of 1812, 169
Wardour Castle, 25

Wareham, 20
Welsh, Richard, 57, 58, 59, 60
Witherington, Pearl, 42
Womens Battalion of Death, 128 et
   seq, 132 et seq, 163

XYZ

Yashka, see Marie Botchkareva
Zelenko, Ekaterina, 163